VB6: YOUR ADO RESOURCE

The Universal Database Power Supply

Richard Edwards

INTRODUCTION

Mention ADO and VB6 and people's eyes get

glossed over

I sincerely hope that this book doesn't cause that to happen.

Welcome to the world of VB6 and ADO!

The purpose of this book is to help you increase your chances of landing a job. I don't pretend that it is perfect. But based on my 7 years working at Microsoft on the phones with customers having issues with databases, I do know that the material covered in this book covers over 90 percent of the resolved issues the customers I dealt with – some 3000 cases – had. The ones I closed with an 87% total satisfaction rating.

Also, I'm not going to tell you that I know everything either. I have little experience with ADODB.Stream – although I have used it once or twice with Active Directory Services.

Things like that are not in this book. Rather, the ADODB Connection, Command And Recordset and their combinations are the ADO objects extensively used in this book.

You are also going to find the core concepts of this book to be in other books in this series on ADO. There are only so many ways you can explain things and I'm not very good at coming up with new and creative ways of saying the same thing more than once.

However, the examples of use will be different in each book and for each language covered. I think example code is what most of you glean from these books anyway.

There are also some key tips and tricks in this book I don't think you'll find anywhere else. You can thank my willingness to tackle some of the hardest issues my customers could come up with for that.

Furthermore, this book is about connecting to all kinds of databases using divers, ISAMS, and providers. And not just for Microsoft's products either. This book also covers connection strings, queries and stored procedures and how you can interact with Access, Excel, Gmail, HTML, Outlook, WBEMScripting and Word.

In-other-words, without going overboard, how you can create databases and tables so you can automate many daily activities using ADO and VB6.

I don't expect you to be a guru after going through this book. But you will be well on your way to being able to confidently walking up to a whiteboard and landing a job based on what is being covered in this book.

I'm not one for long introductions simply because, well, there is a lot to cover in this book and the quicker we go forward with what you need to know, the faster and more confident you will become with what you need to know about ADO to connect seamlessly and effortlessly to a wide collection of database types.

With that said, let's get cracking!

CORE CONCEPTS YOU NEED TO KNOW ABOUT COM AND PROGRAMMING USING VB6

COM Shouldn't be this hard

Which is why I'm using some generic information you will find in all my books dealing with COM – Component Object Model – in all my books dealing with ADO,DAO, ODBC and any other COM related programming techniques.

12 KEYS TO THE KINGDOM

There are 12 lines of code types used today in every language. These are:

1. The creation of an object
2. The use of a property to get\set a value
3. The use of a function that does or does not accept parameters and may or may not return a value. Functions are also called methods.
4. The use of an event that occurs and you write code to respond to it.
5. The use of enumerators
6. The use of conditional Loops
7. The use of conditional branches
8. The use of error trapping
9. Data Conversions
10. Constants
11. Declarations
12. Reg Expressions

These are, of course, not the only ones that compose a VBScript. But they are the ones that help to create a complete program.

Here's what you would normally see:

```
Option Explicit
Dim
Const
CreateObject
Some additional code to create a row and column enumerator.
A way to show or save the information
Closing opened objects
Setting objects equal to nothing.
Sub or functions that helped you along the way.
```

CREATION OF THE OBJECT

Every language that works with Windows and Office products has a way to communicate with them. In VBScript, this is done two ways.

The words here that are used are CreateObject and GetObject.

CreateObject

So, what is CreateObject? The sugar coated answer is that it creates something that can be used to perform a task. In-other-words, if Office is installed, and you typed:

Set oWord = CreateObject("Word.Application")

Once, you've created the object, you have a way to communicate with it.

oWord.Visible = true

CreateObject was modified back around 2000 to include the ability to connect to a remote machine. With all the security and firewalls in place, it is doubtful that would be worth trying today.

GetObject

GetObject is old school. Used to be a time when you could use it for a lot of different things. It works like CreateObject in that you can create an object but is primarily used today with Winmgmts and WinNT.

Set svc = GetObject("winmgmts:\\.\root\cimv2")

Again, once you've created the object, you can use the object reference.

svc.Security_.AuthenticationLevel =6

Please don't try these. They are examples that do work. You'll be able to see them in action much later. There is a lot more to in order to make the above code segments worth your while using.

Besides, creating objects is the fun and easy part of this truly fascinating journey. And like any puzzle, every part that will be covered here is one step closer to completing it.

The use of a property to get\set a value

Properties can be something that you create or something that has already been created for you.

If for example, you decided that a property needed to be set like shown in the above example to 6:

svc.Security_.AuthenticationLevel =6

Okay, so how do you find out what the property was before we changed it?

Dim old

old = svc.Security_.AuthenticationLevel

Yes, it is just that simple.

What if you wanted to create your own property?

First dimension it:

Dim myproperty

Next set it:

myproperty = 25

Next, get it:

Dim old

old = myproperty

Okay, so why would you want to set a property to 25 knowing getting the property would return 25? Well, there are situations where a return value would tell you whether or not something returned with a return value that was greater than zero and if checked, whether or not the call worked

Dim iret

iret = 0

iret = ws.Run("Notepad.exe")

METHODS TO FUNCTION OR TO SUB THAT IS THE QUESTION

What is a method?

A method is a sub or function that can be created by the program to perform a task or called by your program to perform a task that the calling program knows is available and knows how to use it.

Technically, the creation of an object falls under the category of a method as it is a function that returns a value. It is only highlighted a key to the kingdom because of its importance to writing a program.

It is also a way in which zero or more properties can be passed in. These can be set for private or public and they can be a function or a sub.

Function examples:

Function GetValue(ByVal Name, ByVal obj)

End Function

```
Private Function GetValue(ByVal Name, ByVal obj)
End Function
Public Function GetValue(ByVal Name, ByRef obj)
End Function
Sub examples:
Sub SetValue(ByVal Name, ByVal obj)
End Sub
Private Sub SetValue(ByVal Name, ByVal obj)
End Sub
Public Sub SetValue(ByVal Name, ByRef obj)
End Sub
```

When calling a sub or function, unless it is specified as being an optional value, all properties must be satisfied otherwise, the function or sub will either not work or raise an error.

For example, when the below code is called in this manner, it still works:

```
Set locator = CreateObject("WbemScripting.SWbemLocator")
Set svc = locator.ConnectServer()
```

Despite the fact that there are 8 variables that can be passed in:

```
Set svc = locator.ConnectServer(".",  "root\cimV2", Username, Password, Locale, Authority, Security Flags, SWbemNamedValueSet)
```

The reason for these properties being setup this way was simple, unless you are trying to connect to a remote machine, UserName and Password would cause an error. Unless you are going to the default namespace: root\cimV2; and planning on using one of the classes: Win32_LogicalDisk, for example, if the class you are wanting to use is located elsewhere other than the default, you have to specify it before you attempt to use that class.

EVENTS YOU CAN RESPOND TO

Windows in an event driven environment and as such, your VBScript program can create event routines which tell you something has happened, and you can respond to it. Here's an example of an event you can create in code that was created in VBScript that works:

```
Dim w
w = 0
Private    Sub    sink_OnObjectReady(ByVal    objWbemObject,    ByVal
objWbemAsyncContext)
    For Each prop In objWbemObject.Properties_
        v = v + prop.Name & " " & GetValue(prop.Name, objWbemObject) & vbCrLf
```

```
    Next
    MsgBox (v)
End Sub
```

This is called an Async Event call because the program can perform other tasks while waiting for this event to fire off asynchronously.

The problem is, scripts don't just sit around waiting for events to happen isn't what the script likes to do. It likes to do what it needs to perform the task at hand and exit. And that's where we use a bit of VBScript magic.

```
Do While w = 0
    WScript.Sleep(500)
Loop
```

When the Async call, in this case, is completed, the controller of the event raises an event called OnCompleted:

```
Private Sub sink_OnCompleted(ByVal iHResult, ByVal objWbemErrorObject, ByVal objWbemAsyncContext)
    w = 1
End Sub
```

And when this happens the loop that keeps the script running, reads the change in W and knows a w=1 means it is done and the code moves on to do whatever else is left to do.

Also, in some cases Async calls don't need an event function to happen.

Here's another example:

```
Set es = Svc.ExecNotificationQuery("Select * From ___InstanceCreationEvent WITHIN 1 where TargetInstance ISA 'Win32_Process'")
Do While w < 5
    Set ti = es.NextEvent(-1)
    Set obj = ti.Properties_.Item("TargetInstance").Value
        For Each prop In objWbemObject.Properties_
            v = v + prop.Name & " " & GetValue(prop.Name, obj) & vbCrLf
        Next
        MsgBox (v)
        w=w+1
Loop
```

This may appear as though it is not asynchronous, but if you consider the pattern, you can see that the notification isn't just doing it once, it is doing it 4 times and is responding to the event as it happens. And not because you want it to happen 4 times.

Technically speaking there are two of these that VBScript uses. For Each and For

For Each obj in objs
Next
For x=0 To rs.Fields.Count-1
Next

These are technically non-conditional enumerators because they are not based on a conditional which must be proven to be true of false.

For Each is based on a enumerating through as collection of objects. You will be seeing a lot of this kind of enumerator when we work with WBemScripting because the objects collection and the properties collection are a natural fit for this kind of information processing.

The For is also ideal for use with a Fields Count and RecordCount because there is an indexer involved and that allows for easy processing of the information. Unlike For Each, where the collection simply needs to be enumerated through, this also allows us to go to each column and row as a specifically, chosen position rather than blindly look for something in a collection.

For also works with other forms of collected data when working with XML and enumerating through a nodelist, Child Nodes, and Attribute Nodes. Since these too are also index driven.

The use of conditional Loops

There are six conditional loops
Do
Loop Until

Do
Loop While

These two conditional loops are based on the concept that one iteration of the loop must be performed before the evaluation of the condition is said to be true or false.

For example Until(V=1) Even if V was set to 1 from the beginning of the loop, it will proves the code inside that Do statement first. It also assumes the variable will be false during the processing through the loop.

Loop While, on the other hand assumes the conditional statement is true until proven otherwise.

Do Until
Loop

Do While

Loop

These two conditional loops are based on the concept that no iteration of the loop must be performed before the evaluation of the condition is said to be true or false.

For example Do Until(V=1) may already be true and would not even run if it were. It also assumes the variable will be false during the processing through the loop.

Again, the same thing happens with a Do While loop where the conditional statement is true until proven otherwise.

While
Wend

While Statements are conditional too, but it is assumed that while the condition is true, it won't stop processing until the condition is false. I know this sounds the same as a normal do while loop, there is no exit while as there is with a Do while where you can use Exit Do.

The use of conditional branches

Below are conditional branches. Generally speaking these can be stand alone or placed inside a loop.

If Then
End If
If Then
Else
End IF
If Then
Elseif
End If

As an example, below is one of our favorites:
Dim Pos
Pos = Instr(Object.Path_.Classname, "_")

What this does is tell me where the _ is located in a Classname. There are three possible scenarios:

1. There are no _.
2. There is one at the very beginning.
3. There is one in the middle.

If pos = 0 then
Elseif pos = 1 then
Else
End If

This is exactly the logic we needed to parse the three possible incomes from what we knew was going to happen when looking for three specific possibilities.

The use of error trapping

```
On Error Resume Next
If err.number <> 0 then
End If
```

While the use of error trapping is important, it can also mask some issues in programming that you should address otherwise, you'll wind up with a lot of if err.Number <> 0 then statements that are not only ugly looking, they defeat the real reason why you should be using this kind of logic and when.

It is strongly suggested that when you use this kind of error checking it is within the confines of a sub or function where you could place the logic into it to determine whether or not the routine determines if the information is coming in as a specific type.

Suppose your program is running on another machine and that machine doesn't have the object that you want to use. If you use On Error Resume Next at the top of your program without a sub or function to test whether or not the object exists and you have a loop in it, you could find your program running in a loop where that machine uses up all its memory resources and you could be out of a job.

Instead, it is better to create a function that tests whether or not you can create the object and if you can't, then you can call a Wscript.Quit(-1).

Here's an example:

```
Private Function Test_If_Object_Exists(ByVal ObjectName)
    On Error Resume Next
    Set Obj = CreateObject(ObjectName)
    If err.Number <> 0 then
        Err.Clear
        Test_If_Object_Exists = "False"
    Else
        Test_If_Object_Exists = "True"
    End If
End Function
```

When this function is called:

```
Dim iret
iret = Test_If_Object_Exists("DAO.DBEngine.120")
If iret = "False" then
        Wscript.Quit(-1)
End If
```

Had you not written the code this way, and placed the On Error Resume Next inside the at the very beginning of the coding sequence, without error checking, the program would continue trying to run through the everything you told it to do and when it came to a loop, that loop would run and run and run.

Data Conversions

Contrary to popular belief, when you Dim strFirstName, and then used it like it was a string what you're really seeing in VBScript is a Variant. To convert them:

Function	Description
Asc	Converts the first letter in a string to ANSI code
CBool	Converts an expression to a variant of subtype Boolean
CByte	Converts an expression to a variant of subtype Byte
CCur	Converts an expression to a variant of subtype Currency
CDate	Converts a valid date and time expression to the variant of subtype Date
CDbl	Converts an expression to a variant of subtype Double
Chr	Converts the specified ANSI code to a character
CInt	Converts an expression to a variant of subtype Integer
CLng	Converts an expression to a variant of subtype Long
CSng	Converts an expression to a variant of subtype Single
CStr	Converts an expression to a variant of subtype String
Hex	Returns the hexadecimal value of a specified number
Oct	Returns the octal value of a specified number

Suppose I wanted to convert a Variant to Boolean:

```
Dim v
Dim b
v=0
b = Cbool(v)

Msgbox(v)
Msgbox(b)
```
v will return a 0 and b will return False.

Constants

Constants are static values and can be in various formats including Hex and Long.

```
Const wbemFlagReturnImmediately = &h10
Const wbemFlagForwardOnly = &h20
```

These two could just as easily be written like this:

```
Const wbemFlagReturnImmediately = 16
Const wbemFlagForwardOnly = 32
```

We've pretty well covered this. When you Dim – short for Dimension – a variable, by default it is a Variant and we've already shown you how.

```
Dim strQuery
strQuery = "Select * from Products"
```

You can also use the Dim statement to initialize an Array:

```
Dim Names()
Dim Values(,)
ReDim Names(rs.Fields.Count)
ReDim Values(rs.RecordCount, rs.Fields.count)
```

Arrays can also be created by using the ARRAY key word:

```
Dim ComputerNames
ComputerNames = ARRAY("Machine1", "Machine2", "Machine3")
```

Reg Expressions

Regular expressions -- Reg Expressions – are ways in which you can replace string values and validate strings.

Regular Expressions

Arrays

Okay, so here's the idea. Arrays are places where you can store information.

```
Dim x
Dim y
Dim Names()
Dim Values(,)
Redim Names(rs.Fields.count)
Redim Values(rs.RecordCount, rs.Fields.count)
```

This is the way I can create two arrays to hold the names of my fields and the values of my fields when I'm wanting to enumerate through a recordset.

The routine would look like this:

```
y=0
Do While not rs.EOF
  For x=0 to rs.Fields.count-1
      If y = 0 then
      Names(x) = rs.Fields(x).Names
```

```
        Values(y, x) = rs.Fields(x).Value
    Else
            Values(y, x) = rs.Fields(x).Value
    End If
    Call rs.MoveNext()
    y=y+1
Loop
```

These are the core concepts you will need to intelligently write programs in VB6. Beyond this point, we start going into specific details about writing programs that not only work with ADO, DAO, ODBC or any other COM based object including Microsoft Office Products.

The next chapter, we're going to cover the various ways the ADODB.Connection, ADODB.Command and ADODB.Recordset objects can be combined to produce a usable recordset.

CONNECTION STRINGS 101

What makes a connection string work?

What, exactly, is a connection string and why do we use it?

A connection string is a set of properties the ADODB.Connection, ADODB.Command and ADODB.Recordset expect to use when connecting to a database.

But before we get too deep into this chapter, I want to point out a couple of things.

First, the ADODB.Connection is a blank slate container object.

What does that mean?

It means the object itself can not do anything on its own without you supplying it with property values. Yes, by default there are certain properties already set for you but that doesn't mean the connection does any heavy lifting for you.

It simply means someone at Microsoft decided that the ADODB.Connection needed a starting point to make it look fancy and intuitive.

Fact is, not only was ADO a big game changer for Microsoft, it was also a precursor to the .Net framework.

Why do I say this?

Simple, ADO was and is nothing more than a wrapper – just like the .Net Framework has been around existing COM objects – to make it possible that anyone could become a programmer. And that meant that a monkey see, monkey do mentality could be applied. Programming and programmers could be outsourced.

Which is exactly what Microsoft did.

It also galvanized the notion that since anyone could program and coding would be restricted to sets of routines anyone could write in their sleep, the harder work – the new forms of code logic – could be created by ex-Microsoft Employees as a venue for economic growth.

A fancy way of saying – which apparently worked for 7 years prior to the launch of Windows 95 – "What we don't document or provide the resources to complete in the .Net Framework, you insiders can do for us and you stand to make millions from it."

I bring this up because the entire connection string debacle is a perfect example of this.

During my time at Microsoft – from 1996 to 2002 – it took that long to fine tune ADO much less provide us with any documentation on what a provider is, how it works or how to intelligently use it to make a connection string that worked.

In fact, it wasn't until 1999 that anyone really knew how to code the Extended Properties property value correctly in a connection string!

We were being left out of the loop and not for the reason that you might think – our jobs were to be outsourced soon. Nope, that wasn't it.

It was because the higher end consultants either working for Microsoft or independently as Microsoft partners needed to have justification for their existence.

In fact, it got so bad that one disgruntled ex-Microsoft employee created a website devoted to connection strings. Even today, some 20 years later, it is still available on the internet. Here's the link.

Now that you know the truth, we can continue on.

The defaults are based on the use of the MSDASQL provider Or the Microsoft OLE DB Provider for ODBC Drivers. That, in itself, ought to tell you a lot about what ADO really is: a wrapper around the ODBC API.

Furthermore. because it is the default provider, it is the primary reason why you can specify an ODBC Driver without having to include a provider for the connection string. For example, if you want to connect to an older 32-bit Access database, all you have to add to the connection string is: Driver={Microsoft Access Driver (*.mdb)}; and then use the legacy DBQ= and add the location of the database to it. Your connection will work flawlessly.

However, if you do nothing and just want to know what the default properties are of the ADODB.Connection, without calling an open method, just enumerate through the properties and you will expose the below properties:

Provider = MSDASQL

Password =
Persist Security Info =
User ID =
Data Source =
Window Handle =
Location =
Mode =
Prompt = 4
Connect Timeout = 15
Extended Properties =
Locale Identifier = 1033
Initial Catalog =
OLE DB Services = -5
General Timeout =

When we add   Driver={Microsoft Access Driver (*.mdb)} to the connection string, the MSDASQL provider doesn't see the driver as a provider but as Extended Properties:

Provider = MSDASQL
Password =
Persist Security Info =
User ID =
Data Source =
Window Handle =
Location =
Mode =
Prompt = 4
Connect Timeout = 15
Extended Properties = Driver={Microsoft Access Driver (*.mdb)}
Locale Identifier = 1033
Initial Catalog =
OLE DB Services = -5

General Timeout =

From this, can you now see why Extended Properties might be an issue if added to a connection string?

If the connection string looks like this:

cnstr = "Provider=MSDASQL.1;"

How would you add:

Extended Properties= "Driver={Microsoft Access Driver (*.mdb)}; DBQ=C:\Program Files (x86)\Microsoft Visual Studio\VB98\nwind.mdb;"

Since it is already quoted when you set the property without being part of the connection string?

Cn.Properties("Extended Properties").Value = "DBQ=C:\Program Files (x86)\Microsoft Visual Studio\VB98\nwind.mdb;"

Someone on our team figured it out and added double quotes around it:

cnstr= "Provider=MSDASQL,1;Extended Properties=""Driver={Microsoft Access Driver (*.mdb)}; DBQ=C:\Program Files (x86)\Microsoft Visual Studio\VB98\nwind.mdb;"";"

Also, it isn't until we actually call the ADODB.Connection Method: Open that, with the location of the database path and name as part of the connection string that we can see all of the settings this provider exposes:

Data Source =

Window Handle =

Location =

Mode =

Prompt = 4

Connect Timeout = 15

Extended Properties = DBQ=C:\Program Files (x86)\Microsoft Visual Studio\VB98\nwind.mdb;Driver={Microsoft Access Driver (*.mdb)};DriverId=281;FIL=MS Access;MaxBufferSize=2048;PageTimeout=5;

Locale Identifier = 1033

Initial Catalog =

OLE DB Services = -7

General Timeout =

Autocommit Isolation Levels = 4096

And the connection string generated by setting these properties?

cn.Properties("Extended Properties").Value =

"DBQ=C:\PROGRA~2\MIB055~1\VB98\nwind.mdb;Driver={Microsoft Access Driver

(*.mdb)};DriverId=281;FIL=MS Access;MaxBufferSize=2048;PageTimeout=5;;"

cn.Open

Debug.Print "Provider = " & cn.Provider

For Each prop In cn.Properties

    Debug.Print prop.Name & " = " & prop, Value

Next

Debug.Print cn.ConnectionString

Is:

Cn.Connectionstring = "Provider = MSDASQL.1;"

Current Catalog = C:\PROGRA~2\MIB055~1\VB98\nwind

Reset Datasource =

Active Sessions = 64

Asynchable Commit = False

Catalog Location = 1

Catalog Term = DATABASE

Catalog Usage = 13

Column Definition = 0

NULL Concatenation Behavior = 1

Data Source Name =

Read-Only Data Source = False

DBMS Name = ACCESS

DBMS Version = 03.50.0000

GROUP BY Support = 2

Heterogeneous Table Support = 0

Identifier Case Sensitivity = 4

Maximum Index Size = 255

Maximum Row Size = 2096

Maximum Row Size Includes BLOB = False

Maximum Tables in SELECT = 16

Multiple Storage Objects = False

Multi-Table Update = False

NULL Collation Order = 4

OLE Object Support = 1

ORDER BY Columns in Select List = False

Prepare Abort Behavior = 2

Prepare Commit Behavior = 2

Procedure Term = QUERY

Provider Name = MSDASQL.DLL

OLE DB Version = 02.00

Provider Version = 10.00.14393

Quoted Identifier Sensitivity = 8

Schema Term =

Schema Usage = 0

SQL Support = 257

Structured Storage = 1

Subquery Support = 31

Isolation Levels = 4096

Isolation Retention = 0

Table Term = TABLE

User Name = admin

Pass By Ref Accessors = True

Transaction DDL = 8

Asynchable Abort = False

Data Source Object Threading Model = 2

Output Parameter Availability = 4

Persistent ID Type = 4

Multiple Parameter Sets = True

Rowset Conversions on Command = True

Multiple Results = 0

Provider Friendly Name = Microsoft OLE DB Provider for ODBC Drivers

Connection Status = 1

Server Name = ACCESS

Open Rowset Support = 0

Accessible Procedures = True

Accessible Tables = True

Integrity Enhancement Facility = False

Outer Join Capabilities = 83

Stored Procedures = True

Driver Name = odbcjt32.dll

Driver Version = 10.00.14393

Driver ODBC Version = 03.51

Like Escape Clause = N

Special Characters = ~@#$%^&*_-+=\}{"';:?/><,.![]|

Max Columns in Group By = 10

Max Columns in Index = 10

Max Columns in Order By = 10

Max Columns in Select = 255

Max Columns in Table = 255

Numeric Functions = 5439337

SQL Grammar Support = 0

Outer Joins = Y

String Functions = 360061

System Functions = 0

Time/Date Functions = 106495

File Usage = 2

Active Statements = 0

Password =

Persist Security Info =

User ID =

Data Source =

Window Handle =

Location =

Mode =

Prompt = 4

Connect Timeout = 15

Extended Properties =

DBQ=C:\PROGRA~2\MIB055~1\VB98\nwind.mdb;Driver={Microsoft Access Driver (*.mdb)};DriverId=281;FIL=MS Access;MaxBufferSize=2048;PageTimeout=5;

Locale Identifier = 1033

Initial Catalog =

OLE DB Services = -7

General Timeout =

Autocommit Isolation Levels = 4096

Provider=MSDASQL.1;

Cn.ConnectionString = "Provider=MSDASQL.1;"

EXPLORING THE

DATALINKS

DATALINKS HELPS TO RESOLVE SOME ISSUES AND CREATES OTHERS

Perhaps, the least used tool in the arsenal of tools you can use to find out if your provider is DataLinks.

Datalinks will work in both the 32-bit and 64-bit development environments. Meaning, it knows when you're running your programming in 32-bit mode or in 64-bit mode.

To use this tool in VB6, you need create and ADODB.Connection object and then create a DataLinks Object

.

There are two ways to use DataLinks. The first is to Prompt New. This will allow you to either show you what providers are registered as 32-bit or 64-bit or help you build a connection string.

Below is the code to create the DataLinks window:

```
Set cn = CreateObject("ADODB.Connection")
Set dl = CreateObject("DataLinks")

For PromptNew:

Set cn = dl.PromptNew()
For PromptEdit:
Dim cnstr As String
cnstr = "Provider=Microsoft.Jet.OleDb.4.0;Data Source=C:\Program Files (x86)\Microsoft Visual Studio\VB98\nwind.mdb"
cn.ConnectionString = cnstr
dl.PromptEdit(cn)
```

Here's what the DataLinks application looks like in PromptNew mode:

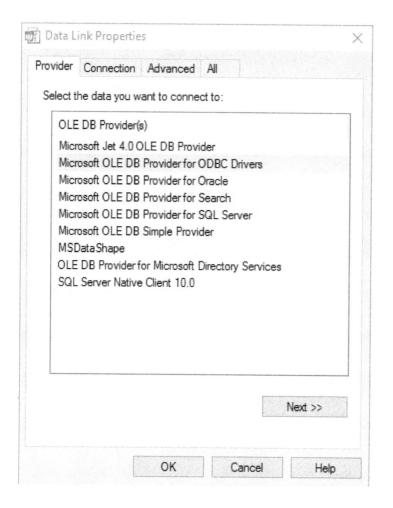

Let's use the same code and see what happens in 64-bit mode.

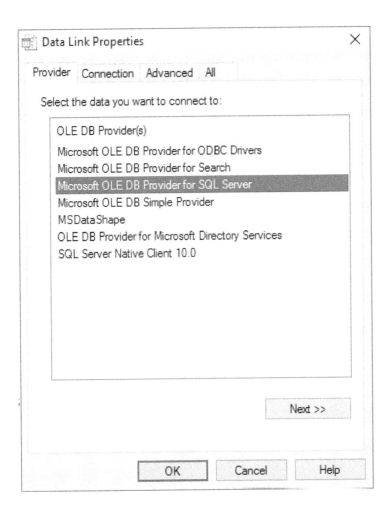

This is what you will see when you want to create a connection string. If you decide to create a connection with the PromptNew call, after the DataLinks window is closed, you can look at the connection string by adding a line:

MsgBox(cn.ConnectionString)

What if you want to modify and test the connection string? Well, that's where the DataLinks.PromptEdit method is used. Below is the code to do this:

Look at the list of providers for 64-bit. Is there a Microsoft 4.0 OLE DB Provider in the list? If you were to try and use a 32-bit version of an OLE DB provider in a 64-bit program, you would get the same error. Let's go back to 32-bit.

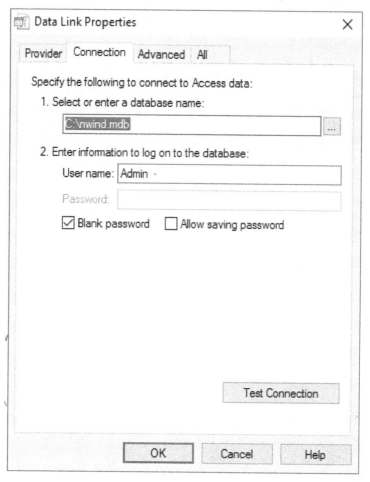

Notice that everything is where it needs to be. The right provider is selected – you can tab over to the Provider and see that it is highlighted – and you see, without tabbing over to the Provider that the location and the name of the database is correctly added to the database text box.

If you want to change the location where the database is located, simply click on the grey button to the right of the database name textbox and you can navigate to where the database would be found.

At this point you can also click on the advanced settings. Unless you're using a network connection, have no interest in setting the connection timeout or want to change the access permission, there's nothing else exposed by clicking the Advanced tab options.

The all tab has a list of all the properties related to the provider and common defaults related to the ADODB.Connection. This includes changing the connection to ODBC and to ISAM driven databases.

You will not normally see these changes. But it is worth spending a couple of pages here to show you what initial properties look like verses the properties that get added once a specific provider is used.

As previously mentioned, by default, the properties for a connection are the following:

> Password
>
> Persist Security Info
>
> User ID
>
> Data Source
>
> Location
>
> Mode
>
> Connect Timeout
>
> Extended Properties
>
> Locale Identifier= 1033
>
> Initial Catalog
>
> General Timeout

Also, by default, the provider is MSDASQL. When a specified provider is used, the entire list changes and incorporates the provider's properties. But this time, instead of having to manually enumerate through all the properties, you can view then using the Datalinks tool and clicking on the All Tab:

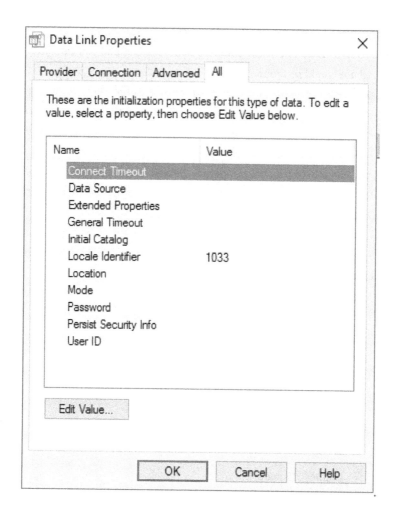

The only difference between the DataLinks View of the properties and the ones listed through our code is the DataLinks View of them ins in alpha-numerical order.

All well and good, but what happens when something other than the default Microsoft Provider for ODBC Drivers is used? The DataLinks becomes demon possessed?

Well, it might look that way considering all the properties that suddenly show up out of nowhere by just clicking a different Provider and then clicking the All tab. Fact is, we would see the same thing happen in code – and probably wouldn't know any better – had we just used a regular connection string, set the provider property to the common Microsoft.Jet.OLEDB.4.0 provider

```
Cache Authentication=True
Encrypt Password=False
Mask Password=False
Password=
User ID=Admin
Data Source=C:\nwind.mdb
Window Handle=0
Mode=16
Prompt=4
Extended Properties=
Locale Identifier=1033
OLE DB Services=-6
Persist Security Info=False
Jet OLEDB:System database=
Jet OLEDB:Registry Path=
Jet OLEDB:Database Password=
Jet OLEDB:Engine Type=0
Jet OLEDB:Database Locking Mode=1
Jet OLEDB:Global Partial Bulk Ops=2
Jet OLEDB:Global Bulk Transactions=1
Jet OLEDB:New Database Password=
Jet OLEDB:Create System Database=False
Jet OLEDB:Encrypt Database=False
Jet OLEDB:Don't Copy Locale on Compact=False
Jet OLEDB:Compact Without Replica Repair=False
Jet OLEDB:SFP=False
Jet OLEDB:Compact Reclaimed Space Amount=0
```

The most interesting thing about this list is the fact that the Jet OLEDB: Engine Type = 0. Why is this? Because we haven't really connected to the database. And, because we haven't, we also don't have all the ADODB.Connection properties.

So, the list that you thought was already longer than your arm, is about to get much longer.

```
Current Catalog
Active Sessions=128
Asynchable Commit=False
Catalog Location=1
Catalog Term=Database
```

```
Column Definition=1
NULL Concatenation Behavior=2
Data Source Name=C:\NWIND.MDB
Read-Only Data Source=False
DBMS Name=MS Jet
DBMS Version=04.00.0000
GROUP BY Support=4
Heterogeneous Table Support=2
Identifier Case Sensitivity=8
Maximum Index Size=255
Maximum Row Size=4049
Maximum Row Size Includes BLOB=False
Maximum Tables in SELECT=0
Multiple Storage Objects=False
Multi-Table Update=True
NULL Collation Order=4
OLE Object Support=1
ORDER BY Columns in Select List=False
Prepare Abort Behavior=1
Prepare Commit Behavior=2
Procedure Term=STORED QUERY
Provider Name=MSJETOLEDB40.DLL
OLE DB Version=02.10
Provider Version=04.00.9801
Schema Term=Schema
Schema Usage=0
SQL Support=512
Structured Storage=9
Subquery Support=63
Isolation Levels=4096
Isolation Retention=9
Table Term=Table
User Name=Admin
Pass By Ref Accessors=False
Transaction DDL=16
Asynchable Abort=False
Data Source Object Thread
ng Model=1
Output Parameter Availability=1
Persistent ID Type=4
Multiple Parameter Sets=True
Rowset Conversions on Command=True
Multiple Results=0
Provider Friendly Name=Microsoft OLE DB Provider for Jet
Alter Column Support=36
Open Rowset Support=2
Cache Authentication=True
```

```
Encrypt Password=False
Mask Password=False
Password
User ID=Admin
Data Source=C:\NWIND.MDB
Window Handle=0
Mode=16
Prompt=4
Extended Properties=
Locale Identifier=1033
Jet OLEDB:System database=
Jet OLEDB:Registry Path=
Jet OLEDB:Database Password=
Jet OLEDB:Engine Type=4
Jet OLEDB:Database Locking Mode=0
Jet OLEDB:Global Partial Bulk Ops=2
Jet OLEDB:Global Bulk Transactions=1
Jet OLEDB:New Database Password=
Jet OLEDB:Create System Database=False
Jet OLEDB:Encrypt Database=False
Jet OLEDB:Don't Copy Locale on Compact=False
Jet OLEDB:Compact Without Replica Repair=False
Jet OLEDB:SFP=False
Jet OLEDB:Compact Reclaimed Space Amount=0
Autocommit Isolation Levels=4096
Jet OLEDB:ODBC Command Time Out=0
Jet OLEDB:Max Locks Per File=0
Jet OLEDB:Implicit Commit Sync=False
Jet OLEDB:Flush Transaction Timeout=0
Jet OLEDB:Lock Delay=0
Jet OLEDB:Max Buffer Size=0
Jet OLEDB:User Commit Sync=True
Jet OLEDB:Lock Retry=0
Jet OLEDB:Exclusive Async Delay=0
Jet OLEDB:Shared Async Delay=0
Jet OLEDB:Page Timeout=0
Jet OLEDB:Recycle Long-Valued Pages=False
Jet OLEDB:Reset ISAM Stats=True
Jet OLEDB:Connection Control=2
Jet OLEDB:ODBC Parsing=False
Jet OLEDB:Page Locks to Table Lock=0
Jet OLEDB:Sandbox Mode=False
Jet OLEDB:Transaction Commit Mode=0
```

Okay, now that you know something about ADO, it is time to look at the ADODB.Connection, ADODB,Command and the ADODB.Recordset as individual objects and them, you're going to see how each can stand alone or work in combinations to get the job done.

OKAY, I NOW KNOW HOW TO CONNECT
What else can I do?

Okay, so we have a connection and you feel confident that your connection string is working. What else do you get from the ADO Connection?

At this point, I can actually imagine the smiles on those of you who know. You have schema information.

What's that? Roughly 27 different calls you can make to discover a whole lot of information about the database. Each provider is designed to support none, some or all of the possible schemas. In the case of the Microsoft.Jet.OleDb.4.0, according to the .Net version of the same thing we should have been able to do from the COM version of the same exact thing, we get 10 supported collections:

```
MetaDataCollections
DataSourceInformation
DataTypes
Restrictions
ReservedWords
Columns
Indexes
Procedures
Tables
Views
```

I could, at this point, perform the same call for each provider I've got available. But are we really interested in all of them at the same time?

Of course not. It is not only impractical; it is the kind of diversion which so many other writers use at this point to get around not pissing of Microsoft and their relationship with Microsoft as Microsoft VIPs. Instead, I'm going to tell you the truth.

The truth is, Microsoft already had plans to go to .Net about the same time I started working for Microsoft – 1996 – because the company knew they wanted to move our jobs overseas and because they made money selling MSDN subscriptions which made MSDN only information appear more accessible to valued customers and not to the average Joe – people like you and me.

In fact, even people like myself who supported database related issues didn't know and weren't allowed to know what constant was used to return a list of all the provider supported schemas.

We had to enumerate through all 27 to know which worked or didn't work. So, in our case, with COM being the way we connected to a database, the below list of usable constants is below:

4	adSchemaColumns
5	adSchemaCheckConstants
6	adSchemaConstraintColumnUsage
8	adSchemaKeyColumnUsage
9	adSchemaReferentialConstraints
10	adSchemaTableConstraints
12	adSchemaIndexes
16	adSchemaProcedures
19	adSchemaStatistics
20	adSchemaTables
22	adSchemaProviderTypes
23	adSchemaViews
27	adSchemaForeignKeys
28	adSchemaPrimaryKeys
30	adSchemaDBInfoKeywords
31	adSchemaDBInfoLiterals

That's a total of 16. Dot Net only exposes 10:

```
MetaDataCollections
DataSourceInformation
DataTypes
Restrictions
ReservedWords
Columns
```

```
Indexes
Procedures
Tables
Views
```

So, based on what we now know, the ADO Connection can tell us a lot about the database we just connected to. But that information is entirely based on what the provider is willing to expose.

Using the JET provider – Microsoft.Jet.OLEDB.4.0 – we can do the following:

```
Dim cnstr As String
cnstr = "Provider=Microsoft.Jet.OleDb.4.0;Data Source=C:\Program Files (x86)\Microsoft Visual Studio\VB98\nwind.mdb"


Dim cn As ADODB.Connection
Dim rs As ADODB.Recordset

Set cn = New ADODB.Connection
cn.ConnectionString = cnstr
Call cn.Open
Set rs = cn.OpenSchema(20) 'get a list of tables

Do While Not rs.EOF()

   For Each Field In rs.Fields
      Debug.Print (Field.Name)
   Next
   Exit Do

Loop
```

Since we're not sure what we're looking for here – okay, I am, but you might not know – the list of field names are listed below:

```
TABLE_CATALOG
TABLE_SCHEMA
TABLE_NAME
TABLE_TYPE
TABLE_GUID
DESCRIPTION
TABLE_PROPID
DATE_CREATED
DATE_MODIFIED
```

Since TABLE_NAME sounds pretty promising, let's take a look at that.

Dim cnstr As String
cnstr   =   "Provider=Microsoft.Jet.OleDb.4.0;Data   Source=C:\Program   Files
(x86)\Microsoft Visual Studio\VB98\nwind.mdb"

Dim cn As ADODB.Connection
Dim rs As ADODB.Recordset

Set cn = New ADODB.Connection
cn.ConnectionString = cnstr
Call cn.Open
Set rs = cn.OpenSchema(20) 'get a list of tables

Do While Not rs.EOF()
    Debug.Print (rs.Fields("TABLE_NAME").Value)
    Rs.MoveNext
Loop

The code produces the list below.

```
Categories
Category Sales for 1995
Current Product List
Customers
Employees
Invoices
MSysACEs
MSysCmdbars
MSysIMEXColumns
MSysIMEXSpecs
```

```
MSysModules
MSysModules2
MSysObjects
MSysQueries
MSysRelationships
Order Details
Order Details Extended
Order Subtotals
Orders
Product Sales for 1995
Products
Products Above Average Price
Quarterly Orders
Sales by Category
Shippers
Suppliers
Ten Most Expensive Products
```

Don't know about you but the list above looks to me lit it includes system tables we don't want and views which we also don't want. So, let's streamline the code output to give us exactly what we want.

```
Dim cn As ADODB.Connection
Dim rs As ADODB.Recordset

Set cn = New ADODB.Connection
cn.ConnectionString = cnstr
Call cn.Open
Set rs = cn.OpenSchema(20) 'get a list of tables

Do While Not rs.EOF()
    If rs.Fields("TABLE_TYPE").Value = "TABLE" Then
      If Mid(rs.Fields("TABLE_NAME").Value, 1, 4) <> "MSys" Then
        Debug.Print (rs.Fields("TABLE_NAME").Value)
      End If
    End If
```

```
        rs.MoveNext
Loop
```

And this produces the following output:

```
    Categories
    Customers
    Employees
    Order Details
    Orders
    Products
    Shippers
    Suppliers
```

To see only the views:

```
Dim cnstr As String
cnstr   =   "Provider=Microsoft.Jet.OleDb.4.0;Data   Source=C:\Program   Files
(x86)\Microsoft Visual Studio\VB98\nwind.mdb"


Dim cn As ADODB.Connection
Dim rs As ADODB.Recordset

Set cn = New ADODB.Connection
cn.ConnectionString = cnstr
Call cn.Open
Set rs = cn.OpenSchema(20)

Do While Not rs.EOF()
    If rs.Fields("TABLE_TYPE").Value = "VIEW" Then
        Debug.Print (rs.Fields("TABLE_NAME").Value)
    End If
```

```
        rs.MoveNext
    Loop
```

And this gives us:

```
        Category Sales for 1995
        Current Product List
        Invoices
        Order Details Extended
        Order Subtotals
        Product Sales for 1995
        Products Above Average Price
        Quarterly Orders
        Sales by Category
        Ten Most Expensive Products
```

We use [] around Tables and Views which have spaces that make them more user friendly. But not so much programmer friendly.

Anyway, the other list of we might want to look at is the Stored Procedures.

```
Dim cnstr As String
    cnstr  =  "Provider=Microsoft.Jet.OleDb.4.0;Data  Source=C:\Program  Files
(x86)\Microsoft Visual Studio\VB98\nwind.mdb"


Dim cn As ADODB.Connection
Dim rs As ADODB.Recordset

Set cn = New ADODB.Connection
cn.ConnectionString = cnstr
Call cn.Open
Set rs = cn.OpenSchema(16)

Do While Not rs.EOF()

    For Each Field In rs.Fields
```

```
        Debug.Print (Field.Name)
    Next
    Exit Do

Loop
```

This code produces:

```
PROCEDURE_CATALOG
PROCEDURE_SCHEMA
PROCEDURE_NAME
PROCEDURE_TYPE
PROCEDURE_DEFINITION
DESCRIPTION
DATE_CREATED
DATE_MODIFIED
```

So, we use the same code we used to get a list of Table Names and modify it to get the stored procedure collection and list all the stored procedure names:

```
Dim cnstr As String
cnstr = "Provider=Microsoft.Jet.OleDb.4.0;Data Source=C:\Program Files
(x86)\Microsoft Visual Studio\VB98\nwind.mdb"


Dim cn As ADODB.Connection
Dim rs As ADODB.Recordset

Set cn = New ADODB.Connection
cn.ConnectionString = cnstr
Call cn.Open
Set rs = cn.OpenSchema(16)

Do While Not rs.EOF()
    Debug.Print (rs.Fields("PROCEDURE_NAME").Value)
    rs.MoveNext
Loop
```

And that gives us this:

```
Alphabetical List of Products
Catalog
```

Customers and Suppliers by City
Employee Sales by Country
Invoices Filter
Orders Qry
Products by Category
Quarterly Orders by Product
Sales by Year
Sales Totals by Amount
Summary of Sales by Quarter
Summary of Sales by Year

And each one of these can be drilled into for the description and definition:

```
Dim cnstr As String
cnstr = "Provider=Microsoft.Jet.OleDb.4.0;Data Source=C:\Program Files
(x86)\Microsoft Visual Studio\VB98\nwind.mdb"


Dim cn As ADODB.Connection
Dim rs As ADODB.Recordset

Set cn = New ADODB.Connection
cn.ConnectionString = cnstr
Call cn.Open
Set rs = cn.OpenSchema(16)

Do While Not rs.EOF()
    If rs.Fields("PROCEDURE_NAME").Value = "Alphabetical List of Products"
Then
        Debug.Print (rs.Fields("DESCRIPTION").Value)
        Debug.Print (rs.Fields("PROCEDURE_DEFINITION").Value)
        Exit Do
    End If
    rs.MoveNext
Loop
```
Which produces:

Description:

Underlying query for Alphabetical List of Products report.

PROCEDURE_DEFINITION:

SELECT DISTINCTROW Products.*, Categories.CategoryName
FROM Categories INNER JOIN Products ON Categories.CategoryID = Products.CategoryID
WHERE (((Products.Discontinued)=No));

This is also a great way to learn how to write queries that you can use to manipulate the tables and learn how to write INNER JOINS, OUTER JOINS and Stored Procedures.

Which brings us to our next chapter.

THE GOOD, BAD AND UGLY QUERY STRINGS

From the simple to the most complex

Queries are the way we ask for information from out tables. The most simple one is:

Select * from Products

This will return all the records contained in the Products table. But what if we don't want all the records returned? What fields would help me limit the amount of records returned from my query?

Well, first, let's take a look at the fields:

```
Dim cnstr As String
cnstr = "Provider=Microsoft.Jet.OleDb.4.0;Data    Source=C:\Program    Files
(x86)\Microsoft Visual Studio\VB98\nwind.mdb"

Set rs = CreateObject("ADODB.Recordset")
rs.ActiveConnection = cnstr
rs.LockType = 3
rs.CursorLocation = 3
rs.Source = "Select * From Products"
Call rs.Open

For Each Field In rs.Fields
   Debug.Print (Field.Name)
Next
```

Which gives us this:

```
ProductID
ProductName
SupplierID
CategoryID
QuantityPerUnit
```

UnitPrice
UnitsInStock
UnitsOnOrder
ReorderLevel
Discontinued

Okay, so we have three IDs: ProductID, CategoryID and SupplierID. And we have a Product state value: Discontinued.

So, the ProductName, UnitPrice, UnitsInStock, UnitsOnOrder and ReorderLevel are all values that a manager of a store would want to keep close tabs on. And, if I were creating this table, I'd probably add a couple of fields to it. Things like ProductShelfLife, InventoryTurnOver and MonthlyDemandUsage come quickly to mind.

Anyway, to use what we have, if I just wanted to know How many Products there are in the table. Next, how many have been discontinued and finally, how many haven't.

```
Dim cnstr As String
cnstr    =    "Provider=Microsoft.Jet.OleDb.4.0;Data    Source=C:\Program    Files
(x86)\Microsoft Visual Studio\VB98\nwind.mdb"

Set rs = CreateObject("ADODB.Recordset")
rs.ActiveConnection = cnstr
rs.LockType = 3
rs.CursorLocation = 3
rs.Source = "SELECT COUNT(ProductID)from Products"
Call rs.Open
Debug.Print (rs.Fields(0).Value)
```

The count returns 77.

```
Set rs = CreateObject("ADODB.Recordset")
rs.ActiveConnection = cnstr
rs.LockType = 3
rs.CursorLocation = 3
rs.Source = "SELECT  COUNT(ProductID)from  Products  where  Discontinued  =
true"
Call rs.Open
Debug.Print (rs.Fields(0).Value)
```

This count returns 8,


```
Set rs = CreateObject("ADODB.Recordset")
rs.ActiveConnection = cnstr
rs.LockType = 3
rs.CursorLocation = 3
rs.Source = "SELECT COUNT(ProductID)from Products where Discontinued =
false"
Call rs.Open
Debug.Print (rs.Fields(0).Value)
```

This count returns 69.

Since these counts are zero based, I subtracted one from each returned value.

All well and good. Let's take a look at that stored procedure.

SELECT DISTINCTROW Products.*, Categories.CategoryName

FROM Categories INNER JOIN Products ON Categories.CategoryID = Products.CategoryID

WHERE (((Products.Discontinued)=No))

ProductID is a Primary Key with the Products table. CategoryID and SupplierID are Foreign Keys with the Products table. When we see things like Categories.CategoryName, we know that specific field names from one table are being combined with another table to create a view from the two or more tables.

In English, this SQL query is saying, I want all the unique records from the products and only CategoryName from Categories where CategoryID from Categories equals Products.CategoryID and where Products.Discontinued= No.

But wait, didn't we just use Discontinued = true or Discontinued = false.

Now, I'm confused. And what's with all those ()?

Turns out the SQL Query returns the same number or rows as did our count: 69 and but the fields came back with a total of 11:

ProductID
ProductName

SupplierID

CategoryID

QuantityPerUnit

UnitPrice

UnitsInStock

UnitsOnOrder

ReorderLevel

Discontinued

CategoryName

CategoryName is the only additional field that was added to the modified returned table. Could we have written the same query another way?

cnstr = "SELECT DISTINCT Products.*, Categories.CategoryName FROM Products INNER JOIN Categories ON Products.CategoryID = Categories.CategoryID WHERE (((PRODUCTS.Discontinued)=No))"

cnstr = "SELECT DISTINCT Products.*, Categories.CategoryName FROM Products INNER JOIN Categories ON Products.CategoryID = Categories.CategoryID WHERE PRODUCTS.Discontinued=No"

cnstr = "SELECT DISTINCTROW Products.* , Categories.CategoryName FROM Products LEFT JOIN Categories ON Products.CategoryID = Categories.CategoryID WHERE Products.Discontinued=No"

cnstr = "SELECT DISTINCTROW Products.* , Categories.CategoryName FROM Products LEFT JOIN Categories ON Products.CategoryID = Categories.CategoryID WHERE (((Products.Discontinued)=No))"

cnstr = "SELECT DISTINCTROW Categories.CategoryName, Products.* FROM Categories RIGHT JOIN Products ON Categories.CategoryID = Products.CategoryID WHERE Products.Discontinued=No"

Okay, so it turns out, you can manipulate these queries and turn them into Stored Procedures. But why do we have inner, left, right and Full Outer Joins in the first place?

Well, as it turns out, there is a reason for all these different kinds of queries.

When I was working with the Games Group at Microsoft, my project was to build a content management program for them so they could manage game testing. I knew each group was called a studio and each studio had projects. These projects could then be broken down into collections known as test packs and test passes. The final table was the test cases themselves.

With studios being the primary key entry, There needed to be an entry for their Projects. However, with many Projects that could be created by a single studio, it made more sense to share the StudioID with the Projects Table rather than try to add Studio entries every time a new Project was added.

So, when the code was written to retrieve the Projects for a specific Studio, All that was needed was the StudioID:

cnstr = "SELECT * FROM Projects WHERE StudioID = " & selectedStudioID & " and WHERE STATUS = 'Active'"

Can you spot the obvious issue here?

Actually, there were three of them.

The first one deals with the fact that Projects can be active or archived. So, there should be Tables made for all archived Projects, Test Passes, Test Packs and Tasks. Without these tables, The active tables would become slow and inefficient.

The second one deals with permissions. For example. without a permissions table, there would be no way to create programs that only those doing task should see.

The third one deals with the logistics of the people who actually perform the tasks of looking for issues in the games. Microsoft calls them TAs or Technical Assistants. They are, indeed, game testers.

This added additional tables that included FTEs and game testers directly wired into the program and interactive with HR information.

It was a lot of work. But one of the most satisfying jobs I ever had as a programmer and it while to program eventually was written in C#, it was my confidence I had built over the years using VB6.

While I would love to cover queries in greater detail, suffice to say, there are some very good books on the subject and, to be honest, this book has a lot of topics to cover.

Okay, so new we know something about the different kind of queries, let's take a look at how queries become store procedures.

WORKING WITH STORED PROCEDURES

What you might not learn from any other book

What, exactly, is a stored procedure?

Well, the best way to describe a stored procedure is that it is a reusable query. Something that you use quite often that you don't want to have to write over and over again. Furthermore, you can call a stored procedure by name. Shouldn't it be much easier to call "Employee Sales by Country" and pass in the different Parameters' values on one line rather then having to write the following over and over again?

```
PARAMETERS [Beginning Date] DateTime, [Ending Date] DateTime;
SELECT DISTINCTROW Employees.Country, Employees.LastName,
Employees.FirstName, Orders.ShippedDate, Orders.OrderID, [Order
Subtotals].Subtotal AS SaleAmount
FROM Employees INNER JOIN (Orders INNER JOIN [Order Subtotals] ON
Orders.OrderID = [Order Subtotals].OrderID) ON Employees.EmployeeID =
Orders.EmployeeID
WHERE (((Orders.ShippedDate) Between [Beginning Date] And [Ending Date]));
```

Also, since we know there are two in parameters, we should be able to get time programmatically, right?

```
Dim cnstr As String
cnstr = "Provider=Microsoft.Jet.OleDb.4.0;Data Source=C:\Program Files
(x86)\Microsoft Visual Studio\VB98\nwind.mdb"
Set cn = CreateObject("ADODB.Connection")
cn.ConnectionString = cnstr
cn.Open
```

```
Set rs = cn.OpenSchema(16)
Do While Not rs.EOF
    Debug.Print (rs.Fields("PROCEDURE_NAME").Value)
    Debug.Print (rs.Fields("PROCEDURE_DEFINITION").Value)
    Debug.Print ("")
    rs.MoveNext
Loop
```

We know from the above code that the Stored Procedure named Employee Sales by Country has two parameters:

PARAMETERS [Beginning Date] DateTime, [Ending Date] DateTime;

So, we should be able to find them when – according to the documentation – the cmd.Paramters.Refresh is used.
Turns out the Microsoft.Jet.OLEDB.4.0 provider returns nothing.

```
Dim cmd As ADODB.Command
Set cmd = CreateObject("ADODB.Command")
cmd.CommandText = "[Employee Sales by Country]"
cmd.CommandType = adCmdStoredProc
cmd.ActiveConnection = cn
cmd.Parameters.Refresh
Dim param As ADODB.Parameter
For x = 0 To cmd.Parameters.Count - 1
    Debug.Print (cmd.Parameters(x).Name)
Next
```

Since there is more than one way to code an Access Connection using ADO, I decided to try using the Driver instead.

```
Dim cnstr As String
```

```
cnstr = "Driver={Microsoft Access Driver (*.mdb)}; DBQ=C:\Program Files
(x86)\Microsoft Visual Studio\VB98\nwind.mdb"

Set cn = CreateObject("ADODB.Connection")
cn.ConnectionString = cnstr
cn.Open

Dim cmd As ADODB.Command
Set cmd = CreateObject("ADODB.Command")
cmd.CommandText = "Employee Sales by Country"
cmd.CommandType = adCmdStoredProc
cmd.ActiveConnection = cn

For x = 0 To cmd.Parameters.Count - 1
    Debug.Print (cmd.Parameters(x).Name)
Next
```

This works and produces the following output:

```
Beginning Date
Ending Date
```

If I really wanted to get granular, I could acquire the Type, Size, and Direction as well. Also, interestingly enough, I didn't have to put the square brackets around the procedure name either.

Anyway, to execute this query, I need to supply the datetime range and use the provider instead of the driver:

```
Dim cnstr As String
cnstr = "Provider=Microsoft.Jet.OleDb.4.0;Data Source=C:\Program Files
(x86)\Microsoft Visual Studio\VB98\nwind.mdb"
Set cn = CreateObject("ADODB.Connection")
cn.ConnectionString = cnstr
cn.Open
```

```
Dim cmd As ADODB.Command
Set cmd = CreateObject("ADODB.Command")
cmd.CommandText = "[Employee Sales by Country]"
cmd.CommandType = adCmdStoredProc
cmd.ActiveConnection = cn

Dim params() As Variant
ReDim params(1)
params(0) = "5/20/1996"
params(1) = "5/31/1996"

Set rs = cmd.Execute(, params)

Do While Not rs.EOF
    For Each Field In rs.Fields
        Debug.Print (Field.Name & " = " & Field.Value)
    Next
    rs.MoveNext
Loop
```

Sample Output:

```
Country = USA
LastName = Leverling
FirstName = Janet
ShippedDate = 5/31/1996
OrderID = 11057
SaleAmount = 45
```

So, with a bit of trial and error, I was not only able to get the parameters for the Stored Procedure, I was also able to use the Stored Procedure to acquire a recordset based on the date range given to the query.

Find this in one of those $40 books or for that matter on the internet that does in fact work.

Let's create some Access Databases.

CREATING ACCESS DATABASES

I'm going to keep this short and sweet as we have a lot to cover and I want to complete this book in time for Christmas.

There are three ways you can create an Access Database using VB6.

First, you can create an Access.Application in VB6 and use the NewCurrentDataBase method to create it. You simply type the following:

```
Set oAccess = CreateObject("Access.Application")
oAccess.NewCurrentDataBase(Path and Name of the new Database, 9)
Or
oAccess.NewCurrentDataBase(Path and Name of the new Database, 10)
Or
oAccess.NewCurrentDataBase(Path and Name of the new Database, 12)
Or
oAccess.NewCurrentDataBase(Path and Name of the new Database, 0)
```

9 creates a 2000 Access Database
10 creates a 2003 Access Database
12 creates a 2007 Access Database
0 creates a Default Access Database

Both the 12 and 0 versions should have the .accdb extension. The 9 and 10, the .mdb extension.

The Second way is to use the DAO.DBEngine. This allows you to create the very earliest version of Access to the latest version of Access.

Below is an example:

```
Set DBEngine = CreateObject("DAO.DBEngine.120")
Set db = DBEngine.CreateDatabase(Path and Name of the new Database,
dbLangGeneral, dbVersion 30)
```

The various versions are listed below.

dbVersion 10 = 1

dbVersion 11 = 8,

dbVersion 20 = 16

dbVersion 30 = 32

dbVersion 40 = 64

dbVersion 50 = 128

The third way is to create an Access Database through code is to use the ADOX.Catalog object.

JET version Engine Type code

JET version	Engine Type code
JET 1.0	1
JET 1.1	2
JET 2.0	3
JET 3.x	4
JET 4.x	5

```
Dim oCat As New ADOX.Catalog
Dim cnstr As String
Dim cn As ADODB.Connection

cnstr = "Provider=Microsoft.Jet.OLEDB.4.0;Jet OLEDB:Engine Type=5;Data Source=C:\store.accdb;"

Set cn = oCat.Create(cnstr)
Call cn.Close
```

THE MECHANICS OF CONNECTING TO A DATABASE

Generic code and possibilities

This chapter is pretty much as simple and to the point as possible. If there are 12 keys to the COM kingdom, there are 3 core ADO objects you will see as examples and use over and over again to connect to almost any database on the planet.

The key here is the connection to the library which gets

You will see the following if you reference a version of ADO. This is called early binding.

ADODB.Connection, ADODB.Command and ADODB.Recordset

```
Dim cnstr As String
cnstr    =    "Provider=Microsoft.Jet.OleDb.4.0;Data    Source=C:\Program    Files
(x86)\Microsoft Visual Studio\VB98\nwind.mdb"

Dim strQuery As String
strQuery = "Select * From Products"

Dim cn As ADODB.Connection
Dim cmd As ADODB.Command
Dim rs As ADODB.Recordset




Set cn = New ADODB.Connection
cnstr= cnstr
cn.Open

Set cmd = New ADODB.Command
cmd.ActiveConnection = cn
```

```
cmd.CommandType = 1
cmd.CommandText = strQuery
```

Use this:

```
'Set rs = cmd.Execute()
'MsgBox (rs.RecordCount - 1)
'MsgBox (rs.Fields.Count - 1)

'or

Set rs = New ADODB.Recordset
Call rs.Open(cmd)
MsgBox (rs.RecordCount - 1)
MsgBox (rs.Fields.Count - 1)
```

This combination produces a forward only cursor. I mention this because you will see the from the MsgBox displaying the recordcount that it comes back with a -1. It also means that you can't edit or update the recordset.

The below code rectifies this situation.

```
Set rs = New ADODB.Recordset
rs.CursorLocation = 3
rs.LockType = 3
Call rs.Open(cmd)
MsgBox (rs.RecordCount -1)
MsgBox (rs.Fields.Count - 1)
```

You will now see a recordcount of 76 and you can now add, edit or delete records from the recordset.

ADODB.Connection and ADODB.Recordset

```
Dim cnstr As String
cnstr   =   "Provider=Microsoft.Jet.OleDb.4.0;Data   Source=C:\Program   Files
(x86)\Microsoft Visual Studio\VB98\nwind.mdb"

Dim strQuery As String
strQuery = "Select * From Products"
```

```
Dim cn as ADODB.Connection
Dim rs as ADODB.Recordset

Set cn = new ADODB.Connection
Cnstr= strCnstr
Cn.Open()

Set rs = new ADODB.Recordset
rs.ActiveConnection = Cn
rs.Locktype =3
rs.CursorLocation = 2
rs.Source = strQuery
Call rs.Open()

MsgBox (rs.RecordCount -1)
MsgBox (rs.Fields.Count - 1)
```

This produces a recordset that records can be added to, edited or deleted.

ADODB.Command and ADODB.Recordset

```
Dim cnstr As String
cnstr   =   "Provider=Microsoft.Jet.OleDb.4.0;Data   Source=C:\Program   Files
(x86)\Microsoft Visual Studio\VB98\nwind.mdb"

Dim strQuery As String
strQuery = "Select * From Products"

Dim cmd As ADODB.Command
Dim rs As ADODB.Recordset

Set cmd = New ADODB.Command
cmd.ActiveConnection = cnstr
cmd.CommandType = 1
cmd.CommandText = strQuery
```

Use this:

```
'Set rs = cmd.Execute()
'MsgBox (rs.RecordCount - 1)
'MsgBox (rs.Fields.Count - 1)

'or

Set rs = New ADODB.Recordset
Call rs.Open(cmd)
MsgBox (rs.RecordCount - 1)
MsgBox (rs.Fields.Count - 1)
```

This combination produces a forward only cursor. I mention this because you will see the from the MsgBox displaying the recordcount that it comes back with a -1. It also means that you can't edit or update the recordset.

The below code rectifies this situation.

```
Set rs = New ADODB.Recordset
rs.CursorLocation = 3
rs.LockType = 3
Call rs.Open(cmd)
MsgBox (rs.RecordCount -1)
MsgBox (rs.Fields.Count - 1)
```

You will now see a recordcount of 76 and you can now add, edit or delete records from the recordset.

ADODB.Recordset

```
Dim cnstr As String
cnstr    =    "Provider=Microsoft.Jet.OleDb.4.0;Data    Source=C:\Program    Files
(x86)\Microsoft Visual Studio\VB98\nwind.mdb"

Dim strQuery As String
strQuery = "Select * From Products"

Dim rs As ADODB.Recordset
Set rs = New ADODB.Recordset
```

```
rs.ActiveConnection = cnstr
rs.Locktype =3
rs.CursorLocation = 2
rs.Source = strQuery
Call rs.Open()

MsgBox (rs.RecordCount -1)
MsgBox (rs.Fields.Count - 1)
```

You will see a recordcount of 76 and you can add, edit or delete records from the recordset.

Mixed Binding is a technique programmers use when they want to make sure their code is written correctly. Once they are satisfied the code is correct, the reference is removed.

ADODB.Connection, ADODB.Command and ADODB.Recordset

```
Dim cnstr As String
cnstr  =  "Provider=Microsoft.Jet.OleDb.4.0;Data  Source=C:\Program  Files
(x86)\Microsoft Visual Studio\VB98\nwind.mdb"

Dim strQuery As String
strQuery = "Select * From Products"

'these get removed once the code is written
Dim cn As ADODB.Connection
Dim cmd As ADODB.Command
Dim rs As ADODB.Recordset



Set cn = CreateObject( "ADODB.Connection")
cnstr= cnstr
cn.Open

Set cmd = New ADODB.Command
cmd.ActiveConnection = cn
cmd.CommandType = 1
```

```
cmd.CommandText = strQuery
```

Use this:

```
Set rs = cmd.Execute()
MsgBox (rs.RecordCount - 1)
MsgBox (rs.Fields.Count - 1)
```

or

```
Set rs = New ADODB.Recordset
Call rs.Open(cmd)
MsgBox (rs.RecordCount - 1)
MsgBox (rs.Fields.Count - 1)
```

This combination produces a forward only cursor. I mention this because you will see the from the MsgBox displaying the recordcount that it comes back with a -1. It also means that you can't edit or update the recordset.

The below code rectifies this situation.

```
Set rs = New ADODB.Recordset
rs.CursorLocation = 3
rs.LockType = 3
Call rs.Open(cmd)
MsgBox (rs.RecordCount -1)
MsgBox (rs.Fields.Count - 1)
```

You will now see a recordcount of 76 and you can now add, edit or delete records from the recordset.

ADODB.Connection and ADODB.Recordset

```
Dim cnstr As String
cnstr  =  "Provider=Microsoft.Jet.OleDb.4.0;Data  Source=C:\Program  Files
(x86)\Microsoft Visual Studio\VB98\nwind.mdb"

Dim strQuery As String
strQuery = "Select * From Products"
```

```
'these get removed once the code is written
Dim cn as ADODB.Connection
Dim rs as ADODB.Recordset

Set cn = new ADODB.Connection
Cnstr= strCnstr
Cn.Open()

Set rs = new ADODB.Recordset
rs.ActiveConnection = Cn
rs.Locktype =3
rs.CursorLocation = 2
rs.Source = strQuery
Call rs.Open()

MsgBox (rs.RecordCount -1)
MsgBox (rs.Fields.Count - 1)
```

This produces a recordset that records can be added to, edited or deleted.

ADODB.Command and ADODB.Recordset

```
Dim cnstr As String
cnstr    =    "Provider=Microsoft.Jet.OleDb.4.0;Data    Source=C:\Program    Files
(x86)\Microsoft Visual Studio\VB98\nwind.mdb"

Dim strQuery As String
strQuery = "Select * From Products"


'these get removed once the code is written
Dim cmd As ADODB.Command
Dim rs As ADODB.Recordset

Set cmd = New ADODB.Command
cmd.ActiveConnection = cnstr
cmd.CommandType = 1
cmd.CommandText = strQuery
```

Use this:

```
Set rs = cmd.Execute()
MsgBox (rs.RecordCount - 1)
MsgBox (rs.Fields.Count - 1)
```

or

```
Set rs = New ADODB.Recordset
Call rs.Open(cmd)
MsgBox (rs.RecordCount - 1)
MsgBox (rs.Fields.Count - 1)
```

This combination produces a forward only cursor. I mention this because you will see the from the MsgBox displaying the recordcount that it comes back with a -1. It also means that you can't edit or update the recordset.

The below code rectifies this situation.

```
Set rs = New ADODB.Recordset
rs.CursorLocation = 3
rs.LockType = 3
Call rs.Open(cmd)
MsgBox (rs.RecordCount -1)
MsgBox (rs.Fields.Count - 1)
```

You will now see a recordcount of 76 and you can now add, edit or delete records from the recordset.

ADODB.Recordset

```
Dim cnstr As String
cnstr = "Provider=Microsoft.Jet.OleDb.4.0;Data Source=C:\Program Files (x86)\Microsoft Visual Studio\VB98\nwind.mdb"

Dim strQuery As String
strQuery = "Select * From Products"
```

```
'this gets removed once the code is written
Dim rs As ADODB.Recordset

Set rs = New ADODB.Recordset
rs.ActiveConnection = cnstr
rs.Locktype =3
rs.CursorLocation = 2
rs.Source = strQuery
Call rs.Open()

MsgBox (rs.RecordCount -1)
MsgBox (rs.Fields.Count - 1)
```

You will see a recordcount of 76 and you can add, edit or delete records from the recordset.

Late binding is used when the programmer knows his or her code and doesn't care about making his or her life easy using intellisense.

ADODB.Connection, ADODB.Command and ADODB.Recordset

```
Dim cnstr As String
cnstr    =    "Provider=Microsoft.Jet.OleDb.4.0;Data    Source=C:\Program    Files
(x86)\Microsoft Visual Studio\VB98\nwind.mdb"

Dim strQuery As String
strQuery = "Select * From Products"


Set cn = CreateObject("ADODB.Connection")
cnstr= cnstr
cn.Open

Set cmd = CreateObject("ADODB.Command")
cmd.ActiveConnection = cn
cmd.CommandType = 1
cmd.CommandText = strQuery
```

Use this:

```
'Set rs = cmd.Execute()
'MsgBox (rs.RecordCount - 1)
'MsgBox (rs.Fields.Count - 1)

'or

Set rs = CreateObject("ADODB.Recordset")
Call rs.Open(cmd)
MsgBox (rs.RecordCount - 1)
MsgBox (rs.Fields.Count - 1)
```

This combination produces a forward only cursor. I mention this because you will see the from the MsgBox displaying the recordcount that it comes back with a -1. It also means that you can't edit or update the recordset.

The below code rectifies this situation.

```
Set rs = New ADODB.Recordset
rs.CursorLocation = 3
rs.LockType = 3
Call rs.Open(cmd)
MsgBox (rs.RecordCount -1)
MsgBox (rs.Fields.Count - 1)
```

You will now see a recordcount of 76 and you can now add, edit or delete records from the recordset.

ADODB.Connection and ADODB.Recordset

```
Dim cnstr As String
cnstr = "Provider=Microsoft.Jet.OleDb.4.0;Data Source=C:\Program Files
(x86)\Microsoft Visual Studio\VB98\nwind.mdb"

Dim strQuery As String
strQuery = "Select * From Products"

Set cn = CreateObject("ADODB.Connection")
Cnstr= strCnstr
Cn.Open()
```

```
Set rs = CreateObject("ADODB.Recordset")
rs.ActiveConnection = Cn
rs.Locktype =3
rs.CursorLocation = 2
rs.Source = strQuery
Call rs.Open()

MsgBox (rs.RecordCount -1)
MsgBox (rs.Fields.Count - 1)
```

This produces a recordset that records can be added to, edited or deleted.

ADODB.Command and ADODB.Recordset

```
Dim cnstr As String
    cnstr  =  "Provider=Microsoft.Jet.OleDb.4.0;Data   Source=C:\Program   Files
(x86)\Microsoft Visual Studio\VB98\nwind.mdb"

Dim strQuery As String
strQuery = "Select * From Products"

Set cmd = CreateObject("ADODB.Command")
cmd.ActiveConnection = cnstr
cmd.CommandType = 1
cmd.CommandText = strQuery
```

Use this:

```
'Set rs = cmd.Execute()
'MsgBox (rs.RecordCount - 1)
'MsgBox (rs.Fields.Count - 1)

'or

Set rs = CreateObject("ADODB.Recordset")
Call rs.Open(cmd)
MsgBox (rs.RecordCount - 1)
MsgBox (rs.Fields.Count - 1)
```

This combination produces a forward only cursor. I mention this because you will see the from the MsgBox displaying the recordcount that it comes back with a -1. It also means that you can't edit or update the recordset.

The below code rectifies this situation.

```
Set rs = CreateObject("ADODB.Recordset")
rs.CursorLocation = 3
rs.LockType = 3
Call rs.Open(cmd)
MsgBox (rs.RecordCount -1)
MsgBox (rs.Fields.Count - 1)
```

You will now see a recordcount of 76 and you can now add, edit or delete records from the recordset.

ADODB.Recordset

```
Dim cnstr As String
cnstr = "Provider=Microsoft.Jet.OleDb.4.0;Data    Source=C:\Program    Files
(x86)\Microsoft Visual Studio\VB98\nwind.mdb"

Dim strQuery As String
strQuery = "Select * From Products"

Set rs = CreateObject("ADODB.Recordset")
rs.ActiveConnection = cnstr
rs.Locktype =3
rs.CursorLocation = 2
rs.Source = strQuery
Call rs.Open()

MsgBox (rs.RecordCount -1)
MsgBox (rs.Fields.Count - 1)
```

You will see a recordcount of 76 and you can add, edit or delete records from the recordset. Please note that all of the above are based on the old Microsoft.Jet.OLEDB.4.0 provider. There are, of course, newer ones for Microsoft

Office all the way up to Version 16 of Microsoft Office 365. The only problem here, of course, is you have to have the 32-bit version of Office installed to use the Microsoft.ACE.OLEDB.16.0 version or below.

VB6 is 32-bit.

Now, let's focus on using ISAMS.

CONNECTING TO A DATABASE USING AN ISAM

The change is in the way the connection string is written

Ever since 1996, the list of ISAMS - indexed sequential access method –

Did you know you can use a wide variety of text files as databases?

It's true, In fact, if you have a table inside a webpage, using the right ISAM or ODBC Driver, you can connect to it and glean from it the table information and convert it into a different type of database format.

Every text file you create will have some kind of delimiter. Otherwise, placing information into a text file would be just another text file and you couldn't reuse the information because there would be nothing a program – including ours – could use to separate one field from another.

These are all various files we're going to be covering, so they really don't change that much. But they are used quite often as data storage and data files.

Of course, CSV or coma delimited is just one of dozens of possibilities. And all of these are fairly easy to code. You enumerate through strNames and strValues and then add the delimiter of choice to separate the fields.

Problem is, it doesn't work. At least, not yet. It will soon. In fact, after I get done with it, you are going to become a master of Delimited files.

ISAMS USED WITH MICROSFT JET OLEDB 3.51

ISAM Engine	Folder Path The Database	File Name The Database	Tables Internal
dBase 5.0	Yes	No	No
dBase III	Yes	No	No
dBase IV	Yes	No	No
Excel 3.0	No	Yes	Yes
Excel 4.0	No	Yes	Yes
Excel 5.0	No	Yes	Yes
Excel 6.0	No	Yes	Yes
FoxPro 2.0	Yes	No	No
FoxPro 2.5	Yes	No	No
FoxPro 2.6	Yes	No	No
FoxPro 3.0	Yes	No	No
HTML Export	No	Yes	Yes
HTML Import	No	Yes	Yes
Jet 2.x	No	Yes	Yes
Lotus WK1	Yes	No	No
Lotus WK3	Yes	No	No
Lotus WK4	Yes	No	No
Paradox 3.X	Yes	No	No
Paradox 4.X	Yes	No	No
Paradox 5.X	Yes	No	No
Text	No	No	No

Suppose, for example, you wanted to open up a dBase III database. Your Data Source would be the folder location where the file resides. The Query would be based on the filename: "Select * From (myDbase.dbf)"

If you wanted to open up an HTML File. Your Data Source would be the Full path to where the file resides: C:\HTML\myhtml.html.

The Query would be bases on the filename: "Select * From (Table1)"

If you wanted to open up a text file. Your Data Source would be the folder location where the file resides. The Query would be based on the filename: "Select * From (Myfile.txt)"

ISAMS USED WITH Microsoft.Jet.OLEDB.4.0:

ISAM Engine	Is The Folder Path The Database	Is The File Name The Database	Are Internal	Tables
dBase 5.0	Yes	No	No	
dBase III	Yes	No	No	
dBase IV	Yes	No	No	
Excel 3.0	No	Yes	Yes	
Excel 4.0	No	Yes	Yes	
Excel 5.0	No	Yes	Yes	
Excel 8.0	No	Yes	Yes	
HTML Export	No	Yes	Yes	
HTML Import	No	Yes	Yes	
Jet 2.x	No	Yes	Yes	
Lotus WJ2	Yes	No	No	
Lotus WJ3	Yes	No	No	
Lotus WK1	Yes	No	No	
Lotus WK3	Yes	No	No	
Lotus WK4	Yes	No	No	
Paradox 3.X	Yes	No	No	
Paradox 4.X	Yes	No	No	
Paradox 5.X	Yes	No	No	
Text	No	No	No	

Below are the various connection strings used for the various ISAMS:

dBase 5.0

cnstr="Provider=Microsoft.Jet.OLEDB.4.0;Extended Properties=""dBase 5.0;hdr=yes;"";Data Source=" + dbpath + ";"

dBase III

cnstr = "Provider=Microsoft.Jet.OLEDB.4.0;Extended Properties=""dBase III;hdr=yes;"";Data Source=" + dbpath + ";"

dBase IV

```
cnstr= "Provider=Microsoft.Jet.OLEDB.4.0;Extended Properties=""""dBase
IV;hdr=yes;"""";Data Source=" + dbpath + ";"
```

Excel 3.0

```
cnstr= "Provider=Microsoft.Jet.OLEDB.4.0;Extended Properties=""""Excel
3.0;hdr=yes;"""";Data Source=" + dbpath + "\" + dbName + ";"
```

Excel 4.0

```
cnstr= "Provider=Microsoft.Jet.OLEDB.4.0;Extended Properties=""""Excel
4.0;hdr=yes;"""";Data Source=" + dbpath + "\" + dbName + ";"
```

Excel 5.0

```
cnstr= "Provider=Microsoft.Jet.OLEDB.4.0;Extended Properties=""""Excel
5.0;hdr=yes;"""";Data Source=" + dbpath + "\" + dbName + ";"
```

Excel 8.0

```
cnstr= "Provider=Microsoft.Jet.OLEDB.4.0;Extended Properties=""""Excel
6.0;hdr=yes;"""";Data Source=" + dbpath + "\" + dbName + ";"
```

HTML Import

```
cnstr= "Provider=Microsoft.Jet.OLEDB.4.0;Extended Properties=""""HTML
Import;hdr=yes;"""";Data Source=" + dbpath + "\" + dbName + ";"
```

Jet 2.x

```
cnstr= "Provider=Microsoft.Jet.OLEDB.4.0;Extended Properties=""""Jet
2.x;hdr=yes;"""";Data Source=" + dbpath + "\" + dbName + ";"
```

Jet 3.x

cnstr= "Provider=Microsoft.Jet.OLEDB.4.0;Extended Properties=""""Jet 3.x;hdr=yes;"""";Data Source=" + dbpath + "\" + dbName + ";"

Lotus WJ2

cnstr= "Provider=Microsoft.Jet.OLEDB.4.0;Extended Properties=""""Lotus WJ2;hdr=yes;"""";Data Source=" + dbpath + "\" + dbName + ";"

Lotus WJ3

cnstr= "Provider=Microsoft.Jet.OLEDB.4.0;Extended Properties=""""Lotus WJ3;hdr=yes;"""";Data Source=" + dbpath + "\" + dbName + ";"

Lotus WK1

cnstr= "Provider=Microsoft.Jet.OLEDB.4.0;Extended Properties=""""Lotus WK1;hdr=yes;"""";Data Source=" + dbpath + "\" + dbName + ";"

Lotus WK3

cnstr= "Provider=Microsoft.Jet.OLEDB.4.0;Extended Properties=""""Lotus WK3;hdr=yes;"""";Data Source=" + dbpath + "\" + dbName + ";"

Lotus WK4

cnstr= "Provider=Microsoft.Jet.OLEDB.4.0;Extended Properties=""""Lotus WK4;hdr=yes;"""";Data Source=" + dbpath + "\" + dbName + ";"

Paradox 3.X

```
cnstr= "Provider=Microsoft.Jet.OLEDB.4.0;Extended Properties="""Paradox
3.X;hdr=yes;""";Data Source=" + dbpath + ";"
```

Paradox 4.X

```
cnstr= "Provider=Microsoft.Jet.OLEDB.4.0;Extended Properties="""Paradox
4.X;hdr=yes;""";Data Source=" + dbpath + ";"
```

Paradox 5.X

```
cnstr= "Provider=Microsoft.Jet.OLEDB.4.0;Extended Properties="""Paradox
5.X;hdr=yes;""";Data Source=" + dbpath + ";"
```

Paradox 7.X

```
cnstr= "Provider=Microsoft.Jet.OLEDB.4.0;Extended Properties="""Paradox
7.X;hdr=yes;""";Data Source=" + dbpath + ";"
```

Text

```
cnstr="Provider=Microsoft.Jet.OLEDB.4.0;Extended
Properties="""Text;hdr=yes;""";Data Source=" + dbpath + ";"
```

This is how you connect to an existing ISAM database. What if you wanted to create one?

Well, you do this:

```
Dim cnstr as String
```

You can either use the ADODB Connection or the Command. We'll use the execCnstr as the string used to export data from the Access Database.

In the case of the ADODB.Connection:

Dim cnstr as String

cnstr = "Provider=Microsoft.Jet.OleDb.4.0;Data Source=C:\Program Files (x86)\Microsoft Visual Studio\VB98\nwind.mdb"

```
Set cn = CreateObject("ADODB.Connection")
cn.ConnectionString = cnstr
Call cn.Open()
```

In the case of the ADODB.Command:

```
Set cmd = CreateObject("ADODB.Command")
cmd.ActiveConnection = cnstr
cmd.CommandType = 1
```

```
Dim execCnstr as String
Dim Path As String
Path = "C:"
```

```
Dim tblName As String
tblName = "Products"
```

```
Dim execCnstr As String
```

dBase 5.0

```
'execCnstr = "Select * Into [dBase 5.0;hdr=yes;Database=" & Path & "\].[" & tblName & ".dbf] from [Products]"
```

dBase III

'execCnstr = "Select * Into [dBase III;hdr=yes;Database=" & Path & "\].[" & tblName & ".dbf] from [Products]"

dBase IV

'execCnstr = "Select * Into [dBase IV;hdr=yes;Database=" & Path & "\].[" & tblName & ".dbf] from [Products]"

Excel 3.0

execCnstr = "Select * Into [Excel 3.0;hdr=yes;Database=" & Path & "\Products.xls].[" & tblName & "] from [Products]"

Excel 4.0

execCnstr = "Select * Into [Excel 4.0;hdr=yes;Database=" & Path & "\Products.xls].[" & tblName & "] from [Products]"

Excel 5.0

execCnstr = "Select * Into [Excel 5.0;hdr=yes;Database=" & Path & "\Products.xls].[" & tblName & "] from [Products]"

Excel 8.0

execCnstr = "Select * Into [Excel 8.0;hdr=yes;Database=" & Path & "\Products.xls].[" & tblName & "] from [Products]"

HTML Export

execCnstr = "Select * Into [HTML Export;hdr=yes;Database=" & Path & "\].[" & tblName & ".html] from [Products]"

Lotus WJ2

```
execCnstr = "Select * Into [Lotus WJ2;hdr=yes;Database=" & Path & "\].[" &
tblName & ".wj2] from [Products]"
```

Lotus WJ3

```
execCnstr = "Select * Into [Lotus WJ3;hdr=yes;Database=" & Path & "\].[" &
tblName & ".wj3] from [Products]"
```

Lotus WK1

```
execCnstr = "Select * Into [Lotus WK1;hdr=yes;Database=" & Path & "\].[" &
tblName & ".wk1] from [Products]"
```

Lotus WK3

```
execCnstr = "Select * Into [Lotus WK3;hdr=yes;Database=" & Path & "\].[" &
tblName & ".wk3] from [Products]"
```

Lotus WK4

```
execCnstr = "Select * Into [Lotus WK4;hdr=yes;Database=" & Path & "\].[" &
tblName & ".wk4] from [Products]"
```

Paradox 3.X

```
execCnstr = "Select * Into [Paradox 3.X;hdr=yes;Database=" & Path & "\].[" &
tblName & ".db] from [Products]"
```

Paradox 4.X

```
execCnstr = "Select * Into [Paradox 4.X;hdr=yes;Database=" & Path & "\].[" &
tblName & ".db] from [Products]"
```

Paradox 5.X

```
execCnstr = "Select * Into [Paradox 5.X;hdr=yes;Database=" & Path & "\].[" &
tblName & ".db] from [Products]"
```

Paradox 7.X

```
execCnstr = "Select * Into [Paradox 7.X;hdr=yes;Database=" & Path & "\].[" &
tblName & ".db] from [Products]"
```

Text

```
execCnstr = "Select * Into [text;hdr=yes;Database=" & Path & "\].[" & tblName &
".csv] from [Products]"
```

And, at this point, The ADODB.Connection after opening the connection uses the following code:

```
Call cn.Execute(execCnstr)
```

And the Command uses:

```
cmd.CommandText = execCnstr
Call cmd.Execute()
```

Now, it is time to talk about using a delimiter other than CSVDelimited. As you can see from the registry entry – I'm running a 64-bit OS –

HKEY_LOCAL_MACHINE\SOFTWARE\WOW6432Node\Microsoft\Jet\4.0\Engines\Te
xt registry entry has a hard wired format type.

Name	Type	Data
(Default)	REG_SZ	(value not set)
CharacterSet	REG_SZ	ANSI
DisabledExtensions	REG_SZ	!txt,csv,tab,asc,tmp,htm,html
ExportCurrencySymbols	REG_BINARY	01
Extensions	REG_SZ	txt,csv,tab,asc
FirstRowHasNames	REG_BINARY	01
Format	REG_SZ	CSVDelimited
ImportFixedFormat	REG_SZ	RaggedEdge
ImportMixedTypes	REG_SZ	Majority Type
MaxScanRows	REG_DWORD	0x00000019 (25)
UseZeroMaxScanAs	REG_SZ	One
Win32	REG_SZ	C:\Windows\SysWOW64\mstext40.dll

There is no way to get around this fact that by default, the Format is going to
be CSVDelimited at the time you create the ISAM driven version of the text file.

However, after it has been created, there is a Schema.ini file that gets created
and that is where we can change the Format. This is what is inside the Schema.ini
file:

```
[Products.csv]
ColNameHeader=True
CharacterSet=1252
Format=CSVDelimited
Col1=ProductID Integer
Col2=ProductName Char Width 40
Col3=SupplierID Integer
Col4=CategoryID Integer
Col5=QuantityPerUnit Char Width 20
Col6=UnitPrice Currency
Col7=UnitsInStock Short
Col8=UnitsOnOrder Short
Col9=ReorderLevel Short
Col10=Discontinued Bit
```

So if I change it to this:

```
[Products.txt]
ColNameHeader=True
CharacterSet=1252
```

```
Format=Delimited(~)
Col1=ProductID Integer
Col2=ProductName Char Width 40
Col3=SupplierID Integer
Col4=CategoryID Integer
Col5=QuantityPerUnit Char Width 20
Col6=UnitPrice Currency
Col7=UnitsInStock Short
Col8=UnitsOnOrder Short
Col9=ReorderLevel Short
Col10=Discontinued Bit
```

And then save the shcma.ini file, when I run the code below to create the text file:

```
Dim cnstr As String
cnstr = "Provider=Microsoft.Jet.OleDb.4.0;Data Source=C:\Program Files (x86)\Microsoft Visual Studio\VB98\nwind.mdb"

Dim strQuery As String
strQuery = "Select * From Products"

Dim cn As ADODB.Connection

Dim Path As String
Path = "C:"

Dim tblName As String
tblName = "Products"

Dim execCnstr As String
execCnstr = "Select * Into [text;hdr=yes;Database=" & Path & "\].[" & tblName & ".txt] from [Products]"
Set cn = New ADODB.Connection
cn.ConnectionString = cnstr
cn.Open


Call cn.Execute(execCnstr)
```

I see the following output:

"ProductID"~"ProductName"~"SupplierID"~"CategoryID"~"QuantityPerUnit" ~"UnitPrice"~"UnitsInStock"~"UnitsOnOrder"~"ReorderLevel"~"Discontinued"

1~"Chai"~1~1~"10 boxes x 20 bags"~$18.00~39~0~10~0

2~"Chang"~1~1~"24 - 12 oz bottles"~$19.00~17~40~25~0

3~"Aniseed Syrup"~1~2~"12 - 550 ml bottles"~$10.00~13~70~25~0

4~"Chef Anton's Cajun Seasoning"~2~2~"48 - 6 oz jars"~$22.00~53~0~0~0

5~"Chef Anton's Gumbo Mix"~2~2~"36 boxes"~$21.35~0~0~0~1

6~"Grandma's Boysenberry Spread"~3~2~"12 - 8 oz jars"~$25.00~120~0~25~0

7~"Uncle Bob's Organic Dried Pears"~3~7~"12 - 1 lb pkgs."~$30.00~15~0~10~0

8~"Northwoods Cranberry Sauce"~3~2~"12 - 12 oz jars"~$40.00~6~0~0~0

9~"Mishi Kobe Niku"~4~6~"18 - 500 g pkgs."~$97.00~29~0~0~1

10~"Ikura"~4~8~"12 - 200 ml jars"~$31.00~31~0~0~0

11~"Queso Cabrales"~5~4~"1 kg pkg."~$21.00~22~30~30~0

12~"Queso Manchego La Pastora"~5~4~"10 - 500 g pkgs."~$38.00~86~0~0~0

So, as you can see, you can customize the Schema.ini file to use what delimiter you want to use once you have a Schema.ini file created. Furthermore, you can have more than one file listed in the Schema.ini file:

```
[Products.csv]
ColNameHeader=True
CharacterSet=1252
Format=CSVDelimited
Col1=ProductID Integer
Col2=ProductName Char Width 40
Col3=SupplierID Integer
Col4=CategoryID Integer
Col5=QuantityPerUnit Char Width 20
Col6=UnitPrice Currency
Col7=UnitsInStock Short
Col8=UnitsOnOrder Short
Col9=ReorderLevel Short
Col10=Discontinued Bit
[Products.txt]
ColNameHeader=True
CharacterSet=1252
Format=Delimited(~)
```

```
Col1=ProductID Integer
Col2=ProductName Char Width 40
Col3=SupplierID Integer
Col4=CategoryID Integer
Col5=QuantityPerUnit Char Width 20
Col6=UnitPrice Currency
Col7=UnitsInStock Short
Col8=UnitsOnOrder Short
Col9=ReorderLevel Short
Col10=Discontinued Bit
```

Furthermore, as long as the schema.ini file is placed in the same folder as the text file and the format of the fields and values are the same, backups of the text file and or adding, editing or deleting contents of the file will appear seamless.

So, now that we have covered what you need to know about ISAMS, it is time to work with the ODBC Drivers.

DATA CRUNCHING
USING ODBC DRIVERS
What you might not learn from any other book

As with Providers, ODBC drivers are created to work with specific type of databases and also come in both 32-bit and 64-bit kinds.

The 32-bit ones can be found in HKEY_LOCAL_MACHINE\SOFTWARE\WOW6432Node\ODBC\ODBCINST.INI\ODBC Drivers. The list here looks like this:

Name	Type	Data
(Default)	REG_SZ	(value not set)
Driver da Microsoft para arquivos texto (*.txt; *.csv)	REG_SZ	Installed
Driver do Microsoft Access (*.mdb)	REG_SZ	Installed
Driver do Microsoft dBase (*.dbf)	REG_SZ	Installed
Driver do Microsoft Excel(*.xls)	REG_SZ	Installed
Driver do Microsoft Paradox (*.db)	REG_SZ	Installed
Driver para o Microsoft Visual FoxPro	REG_SZ	Installed
Microsoft Access Driver (*.mdb)	REG_SZ	Installed
Microsoft Access-Treiber (*.mdb)	REG_SZ	Installed
Microsoft dBase Driver (*.dbf)	REG_SZ	Installed
Microsoft dBase-Treiber (*.dbf)	REG_SZ	Installed
Microsoft Excel Driver (*.xls)	REG_SZ	Installed
Microsoft Excel-Treiber (*.xls)	REG_SZ	Installed
Microsoft FoxPro Driver (*.dbf)	REG_SZ	Installed
Microsoft FoxPro VFP Driver (*.dbf)	REG_SZ	Installed
Microsoft ODBC for Oracle	REG_SZ	Installed
Microsoft Paradox Driver (*.db)	REG_SZ	Installed
Microsoft Paradox-Treiber (*.db)	REG_SZ	Installed
Microsoft Text Driver (*.txt; *.csv)	REG_SZ	Installed
Microsoft Text-Treiber (*.txt; *.csv)	REG_SZ	Installed
Microsoft Visual FoxPro Driver	REG_SZ	Installed
Microsoft Visual FoxPro-Treiber	REG_SZ	Installed
ODBC Driver 17 for SQL Server	REG_SZ	Installed
SQL Server	REG_SZ	Installed
SQL Server Native Client 10.0	REG_SZ	Installed

For the 64-bit versions, these can be found in HKEY_LOCAL_MACHINE\SOFTWARE\ODBC\ODBCINST.INI\ODBC Drivers. The list here looks like this:

Name	Type	Data
(Default)	REG_SZ	(value not set)
Microsoft Access dBASE Driver (*.dbf, *.ndx, *.mdx)	REG_SZ	Installed
Microsoft Access Driver (*.mdb, *.accdb)	REG_SZ	Installed
Microsoft Access Text Driver (*.txt, *.csv)	REG_SZ	Installed
Microsoft Excel Driver (*.xls, *.xlsx, *.xlsm, *.xlsb)	REG_SZ	Installed
ODBC Driver 17 for SQL Server	REG_SZ	Installed
SQL Server	REG_SZ	Installed
SQL Server Native Client 10.0	REG_SZ	Installed

I am only bring this up and showing you because if you have the 32 bit version of Office and the latest build, these 64-bit drivers would be part of the list of 32-bit drivers.

With that said, let's bring in the code needed to use the Access driver and then use the code we used before to create an ISAM database from it.

```
Dim cnstr as String
cnstr = "Driver={Microsoft Access Driver (*.mdb)};DBQ=C:\Program Files
(x86)\Microsoft Visual Studio\VB98\nwind.mdb"""

Dim strQuery As String
strQuery = "Select * From Products"

Set rs = CreateObject("ADODB.Recordset")
rs.ActiveConnection = cnstr
rs.Locktype =3
rs.CursorLocation = 2
rs.Source = strQuery
Call rs.Open()

MsgBox (rs.RecordCount -1)
MsgBox (rs.Fields.Count - 1)
```

As you can see from this code, all the regular variations of connecting to the database works exactly the same way as it did using a provider.

So, all the combinations of ADODB.Connection, Command and Recordset works. Only difference is the connection string – the cnstr – replaces the provider with the driver and the data source with DBQ.

Since unlike the providers there are drivers for the various popular ISAMs. But you still can use the export ISAM databases using the Microsoft Access Driver. Simply use the Driver connection string to open the Access Database and then use the code below to create the ISAM based file.

Below are examples of what is meant.

```
Dim cnstr as String

cnstr = "Driver={Microsoft Access Driver (*.mdb)};DBQ=C:\Program Files
(x86)\Microsoft Visual Studio\VB98\nwind.mdb"

Set cn = CreateObject("ADODB.Connection")
cn.ConnectionString = cnstr
Call cn.Open()
```

In the case of the ADODB.Command:

```
Set cmd = CreateObject("ADODB.Command")
cmd.ActiveConnection = cnstr
cmd.CommandType = 1


Dim execCnstr as String
Dim Path As String
Path = "C:"

Dim tblName As String
tblName = "Products"

Dim execCnstr As String
```

dBase 5.0

```
execCnstr = "Select * Into [dBase 5.0;hdr=yes;Database=" & Path & "\].[" &
tblName & ".dbf] from [Products]"
```

dBase III

```
execCnstr = "Select * Into [dBase III;hdr=yes;Database=" & Path & "\].[" &
tblName & ".dbf] from [Products]"
```

dBase IV

```
execCnstr = "Select * Into [dBase IV;hdr=yes;Database=" & Path & "\].[" &
tblName & ".dbf] from [Products]"
```

Excel 3.0

```
execCnstr = "Select * Into [Excel 3.0;hdr=yes;Database=" & Path &
"\Products.xls].[" & tblName & "] from [Products]"
```

Excel 4.0

```
execCnstr = "Select * Into [Excel 4.0;hdr=yes;Database=" & Path &
"\Products.xls].[" & tblName & "] from [Products]"
```

Excel 5.0

```
execCnstr = "Select * Into [Excel 5.0;hdr=yes;Database=" & Path &
"\Products.xls].[" & tblName & "] from [Products]"
```

Excel 8.0

```
execCnstr = "Select * Into [Excel 8.0;hdr=yes;Database=" & Path &
"\Products.xls].[" & tblName & "] from [Products]"
```

HTML Export

```
execCnstr = "Select * Into [HTML Export;hdr=yes;Database=" & Path & "\].[" &
tblName & ".html] from [Products]"
```

Lotus WJ2

```
execCnstr = "Select * Into [Lotus WJ2;hdr=yes;Database=" & Path & "\].[" &
tblName & ".wj2] from [Products]"
```

Lotus WJ3

```
execCnstr = "Select * Into [Lotus WJ3;hdr=yes;Database=" & Path & "\].[" &
tblName & ".wj3] from [Products]"
```

Lotus WK1

execCnstr = "Select * Into [Lotus WK1;hdr=yes;Database=" & Path & "\].[" & tblName & ".wk1] from [Products]"

Lotus WK3

execCnstr = "Select * Into [Lotus WK3;hdr=yes;Database=" & Path & "\].[" & tblName & ".wk3] from [Products]"

Lotus WK4

execCnstr = "Select * Into [Lotus WK4;hdr=yes;Database=" & Path & "\].[" & tblName & ".wk4] from [Products]"

Paradox 3.X

execCnstr = "Select * Into [Paradox 3.X;hdr=yes;Database=" & Path & "\].[" & tblName & ".db] from [Products]"

Paradox 4.X

execCnstr = "Select * Into [Paradox 4.X;hdr=yes;Database=" & Path & "\].[" & tblName & ".db] from [Products]"

Paradox 5.X

execCnstr = "Select * Into [Paradox 5.X;hdr=yes;Database=" & Path & "\].[" & tblName & ".db] from [Products]"

execCnstr = "Select * Into [Paradox 7.X;hdr=yes;Database=" & Path & "\].[" & tblName & ".db] from [Products]"

Text

execCnstr = "Select * Into [text;hdr=yes;Database=" & Path & "\].[" & tblName & ".csv] from [Products]"

And, at this point, The ADODB.Connection after opening the connection uses the following code:

Call cn.Execute(execCnstr)

And the Command uses:

```
cmd.CommandText = execCnstr
Call cmd.Execute()
```

INTERACTING WITH

EXCEL
Explore the Possibilities

Excel is one of those Microsoft products that has an Achilles' heel. If you have ever had to glean information from it by enumerating through its cells you know exactly what I mean.

To get around this issue and to speed things up dramatically, export the file as a CSV file and read its contents.

I don't know if you have read one of my other books on programming using Python, but I think you are going to find this one a bit different.

I personally wanted to have some fun with this in VB.Net:

```vbnet
Dim v As Long
Dim tempstr As String
Dim Result() As String
Dim l As Long

Set oExcel = CreateObject("Excel.Application")
oExcel.Visible = True

Set wb = oExcel.Workbooks.Add()
Set ws = wb.Worksheets(1)
ws.Name = "Products"

v = 0
Set fso = CreateObject("Scripting.FileSystemObject")
Set txtstream = fso.OpenTextFile("C:\Products.csv", 1,
True, -2)

tempstr = txtstream.ReadLine()
result = tempstr.Split(",")
l= ubound(result) - 1
w = char(65 + l)
ws.Range("A1:" & w & "1") = result
v = 2


Do While txtstream.AtEndOfStream = False
    Dim result1() As String
    tempstr = txtstream.ReadLine()
```

```
        tempstr = Replace(tempstr, char(34), "")
        result1 = tempstr.Split(",")
        ws.Range("A" & v & ":" & w & v) = result1
        v = v + 1
Loop

    ws.Columns.HorizontalAlignment = -4131
    ws.Columns.AutoFit()
```

It took less than 1 second to complete and something tells me that the same amount of time would be required to do the same thing when opening the same file and importing it into Excel.

Below it the code:

```
Set oExcel = = CreateObject("Excel.Application")
oExcel.Visible = True
oExcel.Workbooks.OpenText("C:\Products.csv")
Set wb  = oExcel.WorkBooks(1)
Set ws = wb.Worksheets(1)
ws.Name = "Products"
ws.Columns.HorizontalAlignment = -4131
ws.Columns.AutoFit()
```

The time: 1 second. The results:

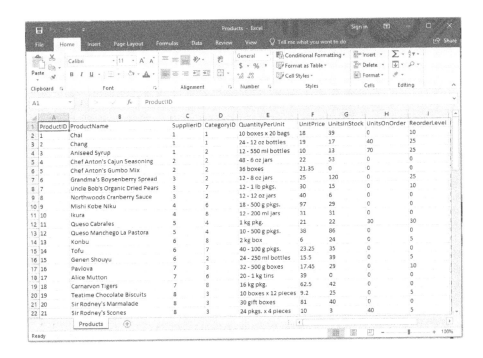

All well and good, but what if I want to import another kind of delimited file? Look at this:

Values	Comments
[string]filename ="C:\\Test\\Excel.txt"	The name of the file you just created
[int]Origin =437	The country code. US is 437
[int]$StartRow =1	Set to 1
[int]DataType = 1	1 = Delimited of 2 =FixedWidth
[int]TextQualifier = 2	-4142 = NoStringDelimiter, 2=", 1 = '
[bool]ConsecutiveDelimiter = false	based on what I've seen, use false. Could cause issues.
[bool]Tab =false	Since this is not, set to true
[bool]Semicolon=false	Since this is not, set to false

[bool]Comma=false	Since this is not, set to false
[bool]Space=false	Since this is not, set to false
[bool]Other=false	Since this is, set to false
[string]Other Char = "~"	Include and end your

If your delimiter was a tab:

Set wb = oExcel.Workbooks.OpenText("C:\Test\Excel.txt",437,1,1,2,False, True, False, False, False, False)

If your delimiter was a Semicolon:

Set wb = oExcel.Workbooks.OpenText("C:\Test\Excel.txt",437,1,1,2,False, False, True, False, False, False)

If your delimiter was a Comma:

Set wb = oExcel.Workbooks.OpenText("C:\Test\Excel.txt",437,1,1,2,False, False, False, True , False, False)

If your delimiter was a Space:

Set wb = oExcel.Workbooks.OpenText("C:\Test\Excel.txt",437,1,1,2,False, False, False, False, True, False)

If your delimiter was Tilde:

Set wb = oExcel.Workbooks.OpenText("C:\Test\Excel.txt",437,1,1,2,False, False, False, False, False, True, "~")

INTERACTING WITH GMAIL

CDO Style

Since all the code variables in this program could be part of your database, the only reason why I am not including it as a recordset is because I believe you have the ability to create the database and add a couple of extra fields to it on your own.

First. Let's take a look at the tested code as a standalone.

```
Dim GMailAccount As String
Dim GMailPassword As String

Dim ToAddress As String
Dim FriendlyFromAddress As String
Dim FriendlyFromName As String
Dim MailSubject As String
Dim MailBody As String

Dim CDOMessage

GMailAccount = ""            'your GMail account
GMailPassword = ""           'your Gmail password
FriendlyFromAddress = ""     'whatever you want to use
```

```
ToAddress = ""                    'who you want to send the mail to.
MailSubject = "Test Mail"
MailBody = "This is a test of the American Broadcasting System. It is only a Test."


Set CDOMessage = CreateObject("CDO.Message")

CDOMessage.Configuration.Fields.Item("http://schemas.microsoft.com/cdo/configuration/sendusing") = 2
CDOMessage.Configuration.Fields.Item("http://schemas.microsoft.com/cdo/configuration/smtpserver")     =
"smtp.gmail.com"
CDOMessage.Configuration.Fields.Item("http://schemas.microsoft.com/cdo/configuration/smtpserverport")
=465
CDOMessage.Configuration.Fields.Item("http://schemas.microsoft.com/cdo/configuration/smtpusessl")     =
True
CDOMessage.Configuration.Fields.Item("http://schemas.microsoft.com/cdo/configuration/smtpconnectionti
meout") = 60
CDOMessage.Configuration.Fields.Item("http://schemas.microsoft.com/cdo/configuration/smtpauthenticate
") = 1
CDOMessage.Configuration.Fields.Item("http://schemas.microsoft.com/cdo/configuration/sendusername")
= GMailAccount
CDOMessage.Configuration.Fields.Item("http://schemas.microsoft.com/cdo/configuration/sendpassword") =
GMailPassword
CDOMessage.Configuration.Fields.Update

FriendlyFromAddress = FriendlyFromName & " <" & GMailAccount & ">"

With CDOMessage
  .To = ToAddress
  .From = FriendlyFromAddress
  .Subject = MailSubject
  .TextBody = MailBody
  .Send
End With


Set CDOMessage = Nothing
Set CDOConfig = Nothing
```

This is about as easy as it can get. Your database table could include timesent, sendmailon, followupdate, response, status, sendhappybirthdayon and other fields that could help you manage bulk mails.

So far so good. What about Doing the same with Outlook mail?

INTERACTING WITH OUTLOOK

Using Outlook.Application

There used to be a time when Outlook Mail was one of the easiest things to do using VB6. You simply added the Microsoft MAPI Controls:

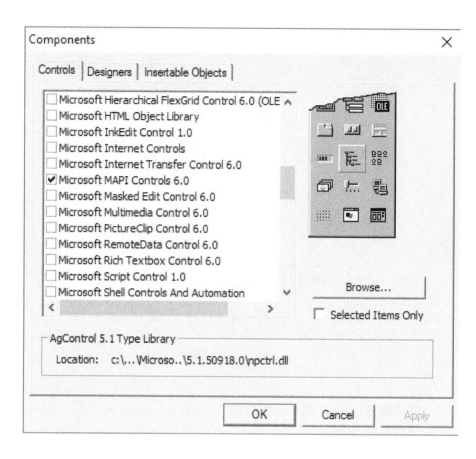

Added them to the form:

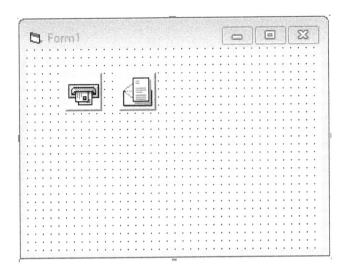

```
Set oOutlook = CreateObject("Outlook.Application")
Set Mapi = oOutlook.GetNamespace("MAPI")

Mapi.Logon("Default OutlookProfile",, False, False)

Set oMail = oOutlook.CreateItem(0)

oMail.To = ""                'Who you want to send mail to
oMail.Subject = ""           'Your subject goes here
oMail.Body = ""              'The body of the message you want to send

oMail.Send()                 'Tell mail you want to send it
oOutlook.Quit()              'Tell Outlook to close
```

The problem is, these controls are 32-bit and if you have the 64-bit version of Office Installed, well, you're not going to be able to use them. So, you have two options. You can install the 32 bit version of Office 2007 – as I did – and discover that unless you're working with a connection the old Office 2007 understands, while the controls work, you still can't do much or use the examples on the internet.

The second option – use CDO like we did with Gmail – is really the best option. Not only because it works but because, to be honest, it is flexible and with a couple of tweaks, the code works flawlessly.

```vb
Dim HotmailAccount As String
Dim HotmailPassword As String

Dim ToAddress As String
Dim FriendlyFromAddress As String
Dim FriendlyFromName As String
Dim MailSubject As String
Dim MailBody As String

Dim CDOMessage

HotmailAccount = ""         'your Hotmail account
HotmailPassword = ""        'your Hotmail password
FriendlyFromAddress = ""    'whatever you want to use

ToAddress = ""              'who you want to send the mail to.
MailSubject = "Test Mail"
MailBody = "This is a test of the American Broadcasting System. It is only a Test."


Set CDOMessage = CreateObject("CDO.Message")

CDOMessage.Configuration.Fields.Item("http://schemas.microsoft.com/cdo/configuration/sendusing") = 2
CDOMessage.Configuration.Fields.Item("http://schemas.microsoft.com/cdo/configuration/smtpserver")     =
"smtp.live.com"
CDOMessage.Configuration.Fields.Item("http://schemas.microsoft.com/cdo/configuration/smtpserverport")
=25
CDOMessage.Configuration.Fields.Item("http://schemas.microsoft.com/cdo/configuration/smtpusessl")     =
True
CDOMessage.Configuration.Fields.Item("http://schemas.microsoft.com/cdo/configuration/smtpconnectionti
meout") = 60
CDOMessage.Configuration.Fields.Item("http://schemas.microsoft.com/cdo/configuration/smtpauthenticate
") = 1
CDOMessage.Configuration.Fields.Item("http://schemas.microsoft.com/cdo/configuration/sendusername")
= HotmailAccount
CDOMessage.Configuration.Fields.Item("http://schemas.microsoft.com/cdo/configuration/sendpassword") =
HotmailPassword
CDOMessage.Configuration.Fields.Update

FriendlyFromAddress = FriendlyFromName & " <" & HotmailAccount & ">"

With CDOMessage
  .To = ToAddress
  .From = FriendlyFromAddress
```

```
    .Subject = MailSubject
    .TextBody = MailBody
    .Send
End With

Set CDOMessage = Nothing
Set CDOConfig = Nothing
```

INTERACTING WITH
MSMQ
Peeking and reading QUEUES

One of my jobs while working for Microsoft was supporting MSMQ or Microsoft Messaging Queue. There are a couple of other IT companies which have their own versions of this type of messaging. IBM comes quickly to mind.

Queues are a way messages are guaranteed to be delivered to the recipients. When properly created, both private and public queues will receive a message from a sender – just like regular mail.

Again, a database can be created to include tables for outgoing and incoming messages. But the first step is to create a queue, send a message to it and then retrieve it from the queue.

Sounds pretty simple, based on what was just said. However, there is a catch. When you read a message from the queue, you also remove it. So, the concept known as peeking into a message is used to assure that processing a queued message is not destroyed through the message enumeration process.

CREATING A QUEUE

Once MSMQ has been installed, you can easily create a queue, send messages to it and read them. Also, adding MSMQ as a service is easy. Use this link for any client based Windows based operating system. Use this link for Windows Servers.

Then, to create a queue, you simply type the following in VB6:

```
Set qinfo = CreateObject("MSMQ.MSMQQUEUEInfo")
qinfo.PathName = ".\private$\TestQueue"
qinfo.Label = "Test Queue"
qinfo.Create
```

INTERACTING WITH WORD

Creating a table from your data in word

Let's suppose, for just a moment, that my boss wants to know what type of BIOS is installed on the 20 computers in the office.

Since this information doesn't change over the lifetime of most motherboards, it is pretty safe to assume that a bios.mdb with tables named by each computer is pretty much going to be the easiest way to grab the data, save it and then generate a report in Word anytime there is a need to create an asset management report on each machine.

The problem is, there are over 27 properties associated with the Win32_BIOS class:

```
class Win32_BIOS : CIM_BIOSElement
{
  uint16  BiosCharacteristics[];
  string  BIOSVersion[];
  string  BuildNumber;
  string  Caption;
  string  CodeSet;
  string  CurrentLanguage;
  string  Description;
  uint8   EmbeddedControllerMajorVersion;
  uint8   EmbeddedControllerMinorVersion;
  string  IdentificationCode;
  uint16  InstallableLanguages;
  datetime InstallDate;
  string  LanguageEdition;
  String  ListOfLanguages[];
  string  Manufacturer;
  string  Name;
  string  OtherTargetOS;
  boolean PrimaryBIOS;
  datetime ReleaseDate;
  string  SerialNumber;
  string  SMBIOSBIOSVersion;
```

```
uint16  SMBIOSMajorVersion;
uint16  SMBIOSMinorVersion;
boolean SMBIOSPresent;
string  SoftwareElementID;
uint16  SoftwareElementState;
string  Status;
uint8   SystemBiosMajorVersion;
uint8   SystemBiosMinorVersion;
uint16  TargetOperatingSystem;
string  Version;
};
```

I'm pretty sure my boss or your boss really doesn't want to know all of this information. Most likely, the Manufacturer, the Name, SerialNumber and InstallDate.

But, I'd rather let him or her decide which properties he or she wants in her report.

```
'Define the path to the target Word file
docName = "<Path_To_The_Word_File>"

'Create new Word object
Set objWord = Sys.OleObject("Word.Application")

'Make Word visible
objWord.Visible = True

'Add new Word dociment
Set objDoc = objWord.Documents.Add

'Print formatted text
Set objSelection = objWord.Selection
objSelection.Font.Name = "Helvetica"
objSelection.Font.Size = "18"
objSelection.Font.Bold = True
objSelection.Font.Italic = True
objSelection.Font.Underline = True
objSelection.ParagraphFormat.Alignment = 1
objSelection.TypeText "First formatted line."
objSelection.TypeParagraph

'Print current date
objSelection.Font.Name = "Arial"
objSelection.Font.Size = "14"
objSelection.Font.Bold = False
objSelection.Font.Italic = False
objSelection.Font.Underline = False
objSelection.ParagraphFormat.Alignment = 0
objSelection.TypeText "Current date: " & Date()
```

```
        objSelection.TypeParagraph

        'Add a table
        Set objRange = objSelection.Range

        '1 row, 2 columns are in the table
        Dim row, col
        row = 1
        col = 2
        objDoc.Tables.Add objRange, row, col

        Set objTable = objDoc.Tables(1)

        'Define a font and style of a table
        objTable.Range.Font.Size = 14
        objTable.Range.Style = "Table Grid"

        'Add a cell with text
        objTable.Cell(1, 1).Range.Text = "This is cell 1"

        'Add a cell with a picture
        objTable.Cell(1,
2).Range.InlineShapes.AddPicture("<Path_To_The_Picture_File>")
        objTable.Cell(1, 2).Range.InsertAfter("This is cell 2 with a picture")

        END_OF_STORY = 6
        objSelection.EndKey(END_OF_STORY)
        objSelection.TypeParagraph()

        objDoc.SaveAs(docName)
        objWord.Quit()
    End Sub
```

INTERACTING WITH WBEMSCRIPTING
Creating records of vital system information

One of the easiest ways of creating records from networked resources is to use what is free and readily available on each one of your computers on your system. The key here is to have administrator permissions on each one of them.

The four basic WBEM – Windows Based Enterprise Management – classes are:

Win32_ComputerSystem

Win32_OperatingSystem

Win32_Process

Win32_Services

In order to connect to a remote Computer – the one you are on doesn't count as a remote computer – you have to create a connection and pass in username and password. That code looks like this:

```
Set l = CreateObject("WBEMScripting.SWbemLocator")
Set svc = l.ConnectServer("Win-7JBE1NVOJBF", "root\CIMV2", "Administrator", "Photo&pro01")
Set objs = svc.InstancesOf("Win32_Process")
For Each obj In objs
    For Each prop In obj.Properties_
        Debug.Print (prop.Name)
    Next
```

Exit For

Next

When I run this code from my local machine, after disabling the firewalls on each one, I get the following:

Caption

CommandLine

CreationClassName

CreationDate

CSCreationClassName

CSName

Description

ExecutablePath

ExecutionState

Handle

HandleCount

InstallDate

KernelModeTime

MaximumWorkingSetSize

MinimumWorkingSetSize

Name

OSCreationClassName

OSName

OtherOperationCount

OtherTransferCount

PageFaults

PageFileUsage

ParentProcessId

PeakPageFileUsage

PeakVirtualSize

PeakWorkingSetSize

Priority

PrivatePageCount

ProcessId

QuotaNonPagedPoolUsage

QuotaPagedPoolUsage

QuotaPeakNonPagedPoolUsage

QuotaPeakPagedPoolUsage

ReadOperationCount

ReadTransferCount

SessionId

Status

TerminationDate

ThreadCount

UserModeTime

VirtualSize

WindowsVersion

WorkingSetSize

WriteOperationCount

WriteTransferCount

INTERACTING WITH HTML

Creating reports from the information collected

WORKING WITH STYLESHEETS

The following couple of pages will show you how the .

Report:

Table

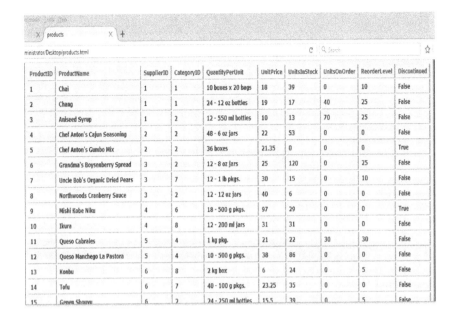

ProductID	ProductName	SupplierID	CategoryID	QuantityPerUnit	UnitPrice	UnitsInStock	UnitsOnOrder	ReorderLevel	Discontinued
1	Chai	1	1	10 boxes x 20 bags	18	39	0	10	False
2	Chang	1	1	24 - 12 oz bottles	19	17	40	25	False
3	Aniseed Syrup	1	2	12 - 550 ml bottles	10	13	70	25	False
4	Chef Anton's Cajun Seasoning	2	2	48 - 6 oz jars	22	53	0	0	False
5	Chef Anton's Gumbo Mix	2	2	36 boxes	21.35	0	0	0	True
6	Grandma's Boysenberry Spread	3	2	12 - 8 oz jars	25	120	0	25	False
7	Uncle Bob's Organic Dried Pears	3	7	12 - 1 lb pkgs.	30	15	0	10	False
8	Northwoods Cranberry Sauce	3	2	12 - 12 oz jars	40	6	0	0	False
9	Mishi Kobe Niku	4	6	18 - 500 g pkgs.	97	29	0	0	True
10	Ikura	4	8	12 - 200 ml jars	31	31	0	0	False
11	Queso Cabrales	5	4	1 kg pkg.	21	22	30	30	False
12	Queso Manchego La Pastora	5	4	10 - 500 g pkgs.	38	86	0	0	False
13	Konbu	6	8	2 kg box	6	24	0	5	False
14	Tofu	6	7	40 - 100 g pkgs.	23.25	35	0	0	False
15	Genen Shouyu	6	2	24 - 250 ml bottles	15.5	39	0	5	False

None:

Black and White

Colored:

AccountExpires	AuthorizationFlags	BadPasswordCount	Caption	CodePage	Comment	CountryCode	Description
			NT AUTHORITY\SYSTEM				Network login profile settings for SYSTEM on NT AUTHORITY
			NT AUTHORITY\LOCAL SERVICE				Network login profile settings for LOCAL SERVICE on NT AUTHORITY
			NT AUTHORITY\NETWORK SERVICE				Network login profile settings for NETWORK SERVICE on NT AUTHORITY
	0	0	Administrator	0	Built-in account for administering the computer/domain	0	Network login profile settings for on WIN-SJRLOAKMF9B
			NT SERVICE\SSASTELEMETRY				Network login profile settings for SSASTELEMETRY on NT SERVICE
			NT SERVICE\SSISTELEMETRY130				Network login profile settings for SSISTELEMETRY130 on NT SERVICE
			NT SERVICE\SQLTELEMETRY				Network login profile settings for SQLTELEMETRY on NT SERVICE
			NT SERVICE\MSSQLServerOLAPService				Network login profile settings for MSSQLServerOLAPService on NT SERVICE
			NT SERVICE\ReportServer				Network login profile settings for ReportServer on NT SERVICE
			NT SERVICE\MSSQLFDLauncher				Network login profile settings for MSSQLFDLauncher on NT SERVICE
			NT SERVICE\MSSQLLaunchpad				Network login profile settings for MSSQLLaunchpad on NT SERVICE
			NT SERVICE\MsDtsServer130				Network login profile settings for MsDtsServer130 on NT SERVICE
			NT SERVICE\MSSQLSERVER				Network login profile settings for MSSQLSERVER on NT SERVICE
			IIS APPPOOL\Classic .NET AppPool				Network login profile settings for Classic .NET AppPool on IIS APPPOOL
			IIS APPPOOL\.NET v4.5				Network login profile settings for .NET v4.5 on IIS APPPOOL
			IIS APPPOOL\.NET v2.0				Network login profile settings for .NET v2.0 on IIS APPPOOL
			IIS APPPOOL\.NET v4.5 Classic				Network login profile settings for .NET v4.5 Classic on IIS APPPOOL
			IIS APPPOOL\.NET v2.0 Classic				Network login profile settings for .NET v2.0 Classic on IIS APPPOOL

Oscillating

Availability	BytesPerSector	Capabilities	CapabilityDescriptions	Caption	CompressionMethod	ConfigManagerErrorCode	ConfigManagerUserConfig
	512	3, 4, 10	Random Access, Supports Writing, SMART Notification	OCZ REVODRIVE350 SCSI Disk Device		0	FALSE
	512	3, 4	Random Access, Supports Writing	NVMe TOSHIBA-RD400		0	FALSE
	512	3, 4, 10	Random Access, Supports Writing, SMART Notification	TOSHIBA DT01ACA200		0	FALSE

3D

Availability	BytesPerSector	Capabilities	CapabilityDescriptions	Caption	CompressionMethod	ConfigManagerErrorCode	ConfigManagerUserConfig	CreationClassName
	512	3, 4, 10	Random Access, Supports Writing, SMART Notification	OCZ REVODRIVE350 SCSI Disk Device		0	FALSE	Win32_DiskDrive
	512	3, 4	Random Access, Supports Writing	NVMe TOSHIBA-RD400		0	FALSE	Win32_DiskDrive
	512	3, 4, 10	Random Access, Supports Writing, SMART Notification	TOSHIBA DT01ACA200		0	FALSE	Win32_DiskDrive

Shadow Box:

Availability	BytesPerSector	Capabilities	CapabilityDescriptions	Caption	CompressionMethod	ConfigManagerErrorCode	ConfigManagerUserConfig	CreationClassName	DefaultBlockSize
	512	3, 4, 10	Random Access, Supports Writing, SMART Notification	OCZ REVODRIVE350 SCSI Disk Device		0	FALSE	Win32_DiskDrive	
	512	3, 4	Random Access, Supports Writing	NVMe TOSHIBA-RD400		0	FALSE	Win32_DiskDrive	
	512	3, 4, 10	Random Access, Supports Writing, SMART Notification	TOSHIBA DT01ACA200		0	FALSE	Win32_DiskDrive	

Shadow Box Single Line Vertical

BiosCharacteristics	7, 10, 11, 12, 15, 16, 17, 19, 23, 24, 25, 26, 27, 28, 29, 32, 33, 40, 42, 43, 48, 50, 58, 59, 64, 65, 66, 67, 68, 69, 70, 71, 72, 73, 74, 75, 76, 77, 78, 79
BIOSVersion	ALASKA - 1072009, 0504, American Megatrends - 5000C
BuildNumber	
Caption	0504
CodeSet	
CurrentLanguage	en|US|iso8859-1
Description	0504
IdentificationCode	
InstallableLanguages	8
InstallDate	
LanguageEdition	
ListOfLanguages	en|US|iso8859-1, fr|FR|iso8859-1, zh|CN|unicode, , , , ,
Manufacturer	American Megatrends Inc.
Name	0504
OtherTargetOS	
PrimaryBIOS	TRUE

Shadow Box Multi line Vertical

Availability			
BytesPerSector	512	512	512
Capabilities	3, 4, 10	3, 4	3, 4, 10
CapabilityDescriptions	Random Access, Supports Writing, SMART Notification	Random Access, Supports Writing	Random Access, Supports Writing, SMART Notification
Caption	OCZ REVODRIVE350 SCSI Disk Device	NVMe TOSHIBA-RD400	TOSHIBA DT01ACA200
CompressionMethod			
ConfigManagerErrorCode	0	0	0
ConfigManagerUserConfig	FALSE	FALSE	FALSE
CreationClassName	Win32_DiskDrive	Win32_DiskDrive	Win32_DiskDrive
DefaultBlockSize			
Description	Disk drive	Disk drive	Disk drive
DeviceID	\\.\PHYSICALDRIVE2	\\.\PHYSICALDRIVE1	\\.\PHYSICALDRIVE0
ErrorCleared			
ErrorDescription			
ErrorMethodology			
FirmwareRevision	2.50	57CE40G	MX4IA3B0
Index	2	1	0

STYLESHEET CODE

NONE

```
txtstream.WriteLine("<style type='text/css'>")
txtstream.WriteLine("th")
txtstream.WriteLine("{")
txtstream.WriteLine("   COLOR: white;")
txtstream.WriteLine("}")
txtstream.WriteLine("td")
txtstream.WriteLine("{")
txtstream.WriteLine("   COLOR: white;")
txtstream.WriteLine("}")
txtstream.WriteLine("</style>")
```

BLACK AND WHITE TEXT

```
txtstream.WriteLine("<style type='text/css'>")
txtstream.WriteLine("th")
txtstream.WriteLine("{")
txtstream.WriteLine("   COLOR: white;")
txtstream.WriteLine("   BACKGROUND-COLOR: black;")
txtstream.WriteLine("   FONT-FAMILY:font-family: Cambria, serif;")
txtstream.WriteLine("   FONT-SIZE: 12px;")
txtstream.WriteLine("   text-align: left;")
txtstream.WriteLine("   white-Space: nowrap;")
txtstream.WriteLine("}")
txtstream.WriteLine("td")
txtstream.WriteLine("{")
```

```
txtstream.WriteLine("    COLOR: white;")
txtstream.WriteLine("    BACKGROUND-COLOR: black;")
txtstream.WriteLine("    FONT-FAMILY: font-family: Cambria, serif;")
txtstream.WriteLine("    FONT-SIZE: 12px;")
txtstream.WriteLine("    text-align: left;")
txtstream.WriteLine("    white-Space: nowrap;")
txtstream.WriteLine("}")
txtstream.WriteLine("div")
txtstream.WriteLine("{")
txtstream.WriteLine("    COLOR: white;")
txtstream.WriteLine("    BACKGROUND-COLOR: black;")
txtstream.WriteLine("    FONT-FAMILY: font-family: Cambria, serif;")
txtstream.WriteLine("    FONT-SIZE: 10px;")
txtstream.WriteLine("    text-align: left;")
txtstream.WriteLine("    white-Space: nowrap;")
txtstream.WriteLine("}")
txtstream.WriteLine("span")
txtstream.WriteLine("{")
txtstream.WriteLine("    COLOR: white;")
txtstream.WriteLine("    BACKGROUND-COLOR: black;")
txtstream.WriteLine("    FONT-FAMILY: font-family: Cambria, serif;")
txtstream.WriteLine("    FONT-SIZE: 10px;")
txtstream.WriteLine("    text-align: left;")
txtstream.WriteLine("    white-Space: nowrap;")
txtstream.WriteLine("    display:inline-block;")
txtstream.WriteLine("    width: 100%;")
txtstream.WriteLine("}")
txtstream.WriteLine("textarea")
txtstream.WriteLine("{")
txtstream.WriteLine("    COLOR: white;")
txtstream.WriteLine("    BACKGROUND-COLOR: black;")
txtstream.WriteLine("    FONT-FAMILY: font-family: Cambria, serif;")
txtstream.WriteLine("    FONT-SIZE: 10px;")
txtstream.WriteLine("    text-align: left;")
txtstream.WriteLine("    white-Space: nowrap;")
txtstream.WriteLine("    width: 100%;")
txtstream.WriteLine("}")
txtstream.WriteLine("select")
txtstream.WriteLine("{")
txtstream.WriteLine("    COLOR: white;")
```

```
txtstream.WriteLine("    BACKGROUND-COLOR: black;")
txtstream.WriteLine("    FONT-FAMILY: font-family: Cambria, serif;")
txtstream.WriteLine("    FONT-SIZE: 10px;")
txtstream.WriteLine("    text-align: left;")
txtstream.WriteLine("    white-Space: nowrap;")
txtstream.WriteLine("    width: 100%;")
txtstream.WriteLine("}")
txtstream.WriteLine("input")
txtstream.WriteLine("{")
txtstream.WriteLine("    COLOR: white;")
txtstream.WriteLine("    BACKGROUND-COLOR: black;")
txtstream.WriteLine("    FONT-FAMILY: font-family: Cambria, serif;")
txtstream.WriteLine("    FONT-SIZE: 12px;")
txtstream.WriteLine("    text-align: left;")
txtstream.WriteLine("    display:table-cell;")
txtstream.WriteLine("    white-Space: nowrap;")
txtstream.WriteLine("}")
txtstream.WriteLine("h1 {")
txtstream.WriteLine("color: antiquewhite;")
txtstream.WriteLine("text-shadow: 1px 1px 1px black;")
txtstream.WriteLine("padding: 3px;")
txtstream.WriteLine("text-align: center;")
txtstream.WriteLine("box-shadow: inset 2px 2px 5px rgba(0,0,0,0.5), inset -2px
-2px 5px rgba(255,255,255,0.5);")
txtstream.WriteLine("}")
txtstream.WriteLine("</style>")
COLORED TEXT

txtstream.WriteLine("<style type='text/css'>")
txtstream.WriteLine("th")
txtstream.WriteLine("{")
txtstream.WriteLine("    COLOR: darkred;")
txtstream.WriteLine("    BACKGROUND-COLOR: #eeeeee;")
txtstream.WriteLine("    FONT-FAMILY:font-family: Cambria, serif;")
txtstream.WriteLine("    FONT-SIZE: 12px;")
txtstream.WriteLine("    text-align: left;")
txtstream.WriteLine("    white-Space: nowrap;")
txtstream.WriteLine("}")
txtstream.WriteLine("td")
txtstream.WriteLine("{")
```

```
txtstream.WriteLine("   COLOR: navy;")
txtstream.WriteLine("   BACKGROUND-COLOR: #eeeeee;")
txtstream.WriteLine("   FONT-FAMILY: font-family: Cambria, serif;")
txtstream.WriteLine("   FONT-SIZE: 12px;")
txtstream.WriteLine("   text-align: left;")
txtstream.WriteLine("   white-Space: nowrap;")
txtstream.WriteLine("}")
txtstream.WriteLine("div")
txtstream.WriteLine("{")
txtstream.WriteLine("   COLOR: white;")
txtstream.WriteLine("   BACKGROUND-COLOR: navy;")
txtstream.WriteLine("   FONT-FAMILY: font-family: Cambria, serif;")
txtstream.WriteLine("   FONT-SIZE: 10px;")
txtstream.WriteLine("   text-align: left;")
txtstream.WriteLine("   white-Space: nowrap;")
txtstream.WriteLine("}")
txtstream.WriteLine("span")
txtstream.WriteLine("{")
txtstream.WriteLine("   COLOR: white;")
txtstream.WriteLine("   BACKGROUND-COLOR: navy;")
txtstream.WriteLine("   FONT-FAMILY: font-family: Cambria, serif;")
txtstream.WriteLine("   FONT-SIZE: 10px;")
txtstream.WriteLine("   text-align: left;")
txtstream.WriteLine("   white-Space: nowrap;")
txtstream.WriteLine("   display:inline-block;")
txtstream.WriteLine("   width: 100%;")
txtstream.WriteLine("}")
txtstream.WriteLine("textarea")
txtstream.WriteLine("{")
txtstream.WriteLine("   COLOR: white;")
txtstream.WriteLine("   BACKGROUND-COLOR: navy;")
txtstream.WriteLine("   FONT-FAMILY: font-family: Cambria, serif;")
txtstream.WriteLine("   FONT-SIZE: 10px;")
txtstream.WriteLine("   text-align: left;")
txtstream.WriteLine("   white-Space: nowrap;")
txtstream.WriteLine("   width: 100%;")
txtstream.WriteLine("}")
txtstream.WriteLine("select")
txtstream.WriteLine("{")
txtstream.WriteLine("   COLOR: white;")
```

```
txtstream.WriteLine("    BACKGROUND-COLOR: navy;")
txtstream.WriteLine("    FONT-FAMILY: font-family: Cambria, serif;")
txtstream.WriteLine("    FONT-SIZE: 10px;")
txtstream.WriteLine("    text-align: left;")
txtstream.WriteLine("    white-Space: nowrap;")
txtstream.WriteLine("    width: 100%;")
txtstream.WriteLine("}")
txtstream.WriteLine("input")
txtstream.WriteLine("{")
txtstream.WriteLine("    COLOR: white;")
txtstream.WriteLine("    BACKGROUND-COLOR: navy;")
txtstream.WriteLine("    FONT-FAMILY: font-family: Cambria, serif;")
txtstream.WriteLine("    FONT-SIZE: 12px;")
txtstream.WriteLine("    text-align: left;")
txtstream.WriteLine("    display:table-cell;")
txtstream.WriteLine("    white-Space: nowrap;")
txtstream.WriteLine("}")
txtstream.WriteLine("h1 {")
txtstream.WriteLine("color: antiquewhite;")
txtstream.WriteLine("text-shadow: 1px 1px 1px black;")
txtstream.WriteLine("padding: 3px;")
txtstream.WriteLine("text-align: center;")
txtstream.WriteLine("box-shadow: inset 2px 2px 5px rgba(0,0,0,0.5), inset -2px
-2px 5px rgba(255,255,255,0.5);")
txtstream.WriteLine("}")
txtstream.WriteLine("</style>")
```

OSCILLATING ROW COLORS

```
txtstream.WriteLine("<style>")
txtstream.WriteLine("th")
txtstream.WriteLine("{")
txtstream.WriteLine("    COLOR: white;")
txtstream.WriteLine("    BACKGROUND-COLOR: navy;")
txtstream.WriteLine("    FONT-FAMILY:font-family: Cambria, serif;")
txtstream.WriteLine("    FONT-SIZE: 12px;")
txtstream.WriteLine("    text-align: left;")
txtstream.WriteLine("    white-Space: nowrap;")
```

```
txtstream.WriteLine("}")
txtstream.WriteLine("td")
txtstream.WriteLine("{")
txtstream.WriteLine("    COLOR: navy;")
txtstream.WriteLine("    FONT-FAMILY: font-family: Cambria, serif;")
txtstream.WriteLine("    FONT-SIZE: 12px;")
txtstream.WriteLine("    text-align: left;")
txtstream.WriteLine("    white-Space: nowrap;")
txtstream.WriteLine("}")
txtstream.WriteLine("div")
txtstream.WriteLine("{")
txtstream.WriteLine("    COLOR: navy;")
txtstream.WriteLine("    FONT-FAMILY: font-family: Cambria, serif;")
txtstream.WriteLine("    FONT-SIZE: 12px;")
txtstream.WriteLine("    text-align: left;")
txtstream.WriteLine("    white-Space: nowrap;")
txtstream.WriteLine("}")
txtstream.WriteLine("span")
txtstream.WriteLine("{")
txtstream.WriteLine("    COLOR: navy;")
txtstream.WriteLine("    FONT-FAMILY: font-family: Cambria, serif;")
txtstream.WriteLine("    FONT-SIZE: 12px;")
txtstream.WriteLine("    text-align: left;")
txtstream.WriteLine("    white-Space: nowrap;")
txtstream.WriteLine("    width: 100%;")
txtstream.WriteLine("}")
txtstream.WriteLine("textarea")
txtstream.WriteLine("{")
txtstream.WriteLine("    COLOR: navy;")
txtstream.WriteLine("    FONT-FAMILY: font-family: Cambria, serif;")
txtstream.WriteLine("    FONT-SIZE: 12px;")
txtstream.WriteLine("    text-align: left;")
txtstream.WriteLine("    white-Space: nowrap;")
txtstream.WriteLine("    display:inline-block;")
txtstream.WriteLine("    width: 100%;")
txtstream.WriteLine("}")
txtstream.WriteLine("select")
txtstream.WriteLine("{")
txtstream.WriteLine("    COLOR: navy;")
txtstream.WriteLine("    FONT-FAMILY: font-family: Cambria, serif;")
```

```
txtstream.WriteLine("    FONT-SIZE: 10px;")
txtstream.WriteLine("    text-align: left;")
txtstream.WriteLine("    white-Space: nowrap;")
txtstream.WriteLine("    display:inline-block;")
txtstream.WriteLine("    width: 100%;")
txtstream.WriteLine("}")
txtstream.WriteLine("input")
txtstream.WriteLine("{")
txtstream.WriteLine("    COLOR: navy;")
txtstream.WriteLine("    FONT-FAMILY: font-family: Cambria, serif;")
txtstream.WriteLine("    FONT-SIZE: 12px;")
txtstream.WriteLine("    text-align: left;")
txtstream.WriteLine("    display:table-cell;")
txtstream.WriteLine("    white-Space: nowrap;")
txtstream.WriteLine("}")
txtstream.WriteLine("h1 {")
txtstream.WriteLine("color: antiquewhite;")
txtstream.WriteLine("text-shadow: 1px 1px 1px black;")
txtstream.WriteLine("padding: 3px;")
txtstream.WriteLine("text-align: center;")
txtstream.WriteLine("box-shadow: inset 2px 2px 5px rgba(0,0,0,0.5), inset -2px
-2px 5px rgba(255,255,255,0.5);")
txtstream.WriteLine("}")
txtstream.WriteLine("tr:nth-child(even){background-color:#f2f2f2;}")
txtstream.WriteLine("tr:nth-child(odd){background-color:#cccccc;
color:#f2f2f2;}")
txtstream.WriteLine("</style>")
```

GHOST DECORATED

```
txtstream.WriteLine("<style type='text/css'>")
txtstream.WriteLine("th")
txtstream.WriteLine("{")
txtstream.WriteLine("    COLOR: black;")
txtstream.WriteLine("    BACKGROUND-COLOR: white;")
txtstream.WriteLine("    FONT-FAMILY:font-family: Cambria, serif;")
txtstream.WriteLine("    FONT-SIZE: 12px;")
txtstream.WriteLine("    text-align: left;")
txtstream.WriteLine("    white-Space: nowrap;")
txtstream.WriteLine("}")
```

```
txtstream.WriteLine("td")
txtstream.WriteLine("{")
txtstream.WriteLine("   COLOR: black;")
txtstream.WriteLine("   BACKGROUND-COLOR: white;")
txtstream.WriteLine("   FONT-FAMILY: font-family: Cambria, serif;")
txtstream.WriteLine("   FONT-SIZE: 12px;")
txtstream.WriteLine("   text-align: left;")
txtstream.WriteLine("   white-Space: nowrap;")
txtstream.WriteLine("}")
txtstream.WriteLine("div")
txtstream.WriteLine("{")
txtstream.WriteLine("   COLOR: black;")
txtstream.WriteLine("   BACKGROUND-COLOR: white;")
txtstream.WriteLine("   FONT-FAMILY: font-family: Cambria, serif;")
txtstream.WriteLine("   FONT-SIZE: 10px;")
txtstream.WriteLine("   text-align: left;")
txtstream.WriteLine("   white-Space: nowrap;")
txtstream.WriteLine("}")
txtstream.WriteLine("span")
txtstream.WriteLine("{")
txtstream.WriteLine("   COLOR: black;")
txtstream.WriteLine("   BACKGROUND-COLOR: white;")
txtstream.WriteLine("   FONT-FAMILY: font-family: Cambria, serif;")
txtstream.WriteLine("   FONT-SIZE: 10px;")
txtstream.WriteLine("   text-align: left;")
txtstream.WriteLine("   white-Space: nowrap;")
txtstream.WriteLine("   display:inline-block;")
txtstream.WriteLine("   width: 100%;")
txtstream.WriteLine("}")
txtstream.WriteLine("textarea")
txtstream.WriteLine("{")
txtstream.WriteLine("   COLOR: black;")
txtstream.WriteLine("   BACKGROUND-COLOR: white;")
txtstream.WriteLine("   FONT-FAMILY: font-family: Cambria, serif;")
txtstream.WriteLine("   FONT-SIZE: 10px;")
txtstream.WriteLine("   text-align: left;")
txtstream.WriteLine("   white-Space: nowrap;")
txtstream.WriteLine("   width: 100%;")
txtstream.WriteLine("}")
txtstream.WriteLine("select")
```

```
txtstream.WriteLine("{")
txtstream.WriteLine("   COLOR: black;")
txtstream.WriteLine("   BACKGROUND-COLOR: white;")
txtstream.WriteLine("   FONT-FAMILY: font-family: Cambria, serif;")
txtstream.WriteLine("   FONT-SIZE: 10px;")
txtstream.WriteLine("   text-align: left;")
txtstream.WriteLine("   white-Space: nowrap;")
txtstream.WriteLine("   width: 100%;")
txtstream.WriteLine("}")
txtstream.WriteLine("input")
txtstream.WriteLine("{")
txtstream.WriteLine("   COLOR: black;")
txtstream.WriteLine("   BACKGROUND-COLOR: white;")
txtstream.WriteLine("   FONT-FAMILY: font-family: Cambria, serif;")
txtstream.WriteLine("   FONT-SIZE: 12px;")
txtstream.WriteLine("   text-align: left;")
txtstream.WriteLine("   display:table-cell;")
txtstream.WriteLine("   white-Space: nowrap;")
txtstream.WriteLine("}")
txtstream.WriteLine("h1 {")
txtstream.WriteLine("color: antiquewhite;")
txtstream.WriteLine("text-shadow: 1px 1px 1px black;")
txtstream.WriteLine("padding: 3px;")
txtstream.WriteLine("text-align: center;")
txtstream.WriteLine("box-shadow: inset 2px 2px 5px rgba(0,0,0,0.5), inset -2px
-2px 5px rgba(255,255,255,0.5);")
txtstream.WriteLine("}")
txtstream.WriteLine("</style>")
```

3D


```
txtstream.WriteLine("<style type='text/css'>")
txtstream.WriteLine("body")
txtstream.WriteLine("{")
txtstream.WriteLine("   PADDING-RIGHT: 0px;")
txtstream.WriteLine("   PADDING-LEFT: 0px;")
txtstream.WriteLine("   PADDING-BOTTOM: 0px;")
txtstream.WriteLine("   MARGIN: 0px;")
txtstream.WriteLine("   COLOR: #333;")
```

```
txtstream.WriteLine("   PADDING-TOP: 0px;")
txtstream.WriteLine("   FONT-FAMILY: verdana, arial, helvetica, sans-serif;")
txtstream.WriteLine("}")
txtstream.WriteLine("table")
txtstream.WriteLine("{")
txtstream.WriteLine("   BORDER-RIGHT: #999999 3px solid;")
txtstream.WriteLine("   PADDING-RIGHT: 6px;")
txtstream.WriteLine("   PADDING-LEFT: 6px;")
txtstream.WriteLine("   FONT-WEIGHT: Bold;")
txtstream.WriteLine("   FONT-SIZE: 14px;")
txtstream.WriteLine("   PADDING-BOTTOM: 6px;")
txtstream.WriteLine("   COLOR: Peru;")
txtstream.WriteLine("   LINE-HEIGHT: 14px;")
txtstream.WriteLine("   PADDING-TOP: 6px;")
txtstream.WriteLine("   BORDER-BOTTOM: #999 1px solid;")
txtstream.WriteLine("   BACKGROUND-COLOR: #eeeeee;")
txtstream.WriteLine("   FONT-FAMILY: verdana, arial, helvetica, sans-serif;")
txtstream.WriteLine("   FONT-SIZE: 12px;")
txtstream.WriteLine("}")
txtstream.WriteLine("th")
txtstream.WriteLine("{")
txtstream.WriteLine("   BORDER-RIGHT: #999999 3px solid;")
txtstream.WriteLine("   PADDING-RIGHT: 6px;")
txtstream.WriteLine("   PADDING-LEFT: 6px;")
txtstream.WriteLine("   FONT-WEIGHT: Bold;")
txtstream.WriteLine("   FONT-SIZE: 14px;")
txtstream.WriteLine("   PADDING-BOTTOM: 6px;")
txtstream.WriteLine("   COLOR: darkred;")
txtstream.WriteLine("   LINE-HEIGHT: 14px;")
txtstream.WriteLine("   PADDING-TOP: 6px;")
txtstream.WriteLine("   BORDER-BOTTOM: #999 1px solid;")
txtstream.WriteLine("   BACKGROUND-COLOR: #eeeeee;")
txtstream.WriteLine("   FONT-FAMILY:font-family: Cambria, serif;")
txtstream.WriteLine("   FONT-SIZE: 12px;")
txtstream.WriteLine("   text-align: left;")
txtstream.WriteLine("   white-Space: nowrap;")
txtstream.WriteLine("}")
txtstream.WriteLine(".th")
txtstream.WriteLine("{")
txtstream.WriteLine("   BORDER-RIGHT: #999999 2px solid;")
```

```
txtstream.WriteLine("    PADDING-RIGHT: 6px;")
txtstream.WriteLine("    PADDING-LEFT: 6px;")
txtstream.WriteLine("    FONT-WEIGHT: Bold;")
txtstream.WriteLine("    PADDING-BOTTOM: 6px;")
txtstream.WriteLine("    COLOR: black;")
txtstream.WriteLine("    PADDING-TOP: 6px;")
txtstream.WriteLine("    BORDER-BOTTOM: #999 2px solid;")
txtstream.WriteLine("    BACKGROUND-COLOR: #eeeeee;")
txtstream.WriteLine("    FONT-FAMILY: font-family: Cambria, serif;")
txtstream.WriteLine("    FONT-SIZE: 10px;")
txtstream.WriteLine("    text-align: right;")
txtstream.WriteLine("    white-Space: nowrap;")
txtstream.WriteLine("}")
txtstream.WriteLine("td")
txtstream.WriteLine("{")
txtstream.WriteLine("    BORDER-RIGHT: #999999 3px solid;")
txtstream.WriteLine("    PADDING-RIGHT: 6px;")
txtstream.WriteLine("    PADDING-LEFT: 6px;")
txtstream.WriteLine("    FONT-WEIGHT: Normal;")
txtstream.WriteLine("    PADDING-BOTTOM: 6px;")
txtstream.WriteLine("    COLOR: navy;")
txtstream.WriteLine("    LINE-HEIGHT: 14px;")
txtstream.WriteLine("    PADDING-TOP: 6px;")
txtstream.WriteLine("    BORDER-BOTTOM: #999 1px solid;")
txtstream.WriteLine("    BACKGROUND-COLOR: #eeeeee;")
txtstream.WriteLine("    FONT-FAMILY: font-family: Cambria, serif;")
txtstream.WriteLine("    FONT-SIZE: 12px;")
txtstream.WriteLine("    text-align: left;")
txtstream.WriteLine("    white-Space: nowrap;")
txtstream.WriteLine("}")
txtstream.WriteLine("div")
txtstream.WriteLine("{")
txtstream.WriteLine("    BORDER-RIGHT: #999999 3px solid;")
txtstream.WriteLine("    PADDING-RIGHT: 6px;")
txtstream.WriteLine("    PADDING-LEFT: 6px;")
txtstream.WriteLine("    FONT-WEIGHT: Normal;")
txtstream.WriteLine("    PADDING-BOTTOM: 6px;")
txtstream.WriteLine("    COLOR: white;")
txtstream.WriteLine("    PADDING-TOP: 6px;")
txtstream.WriteLine("    BORDER-BOTTOM: #999 1px solid;")
```

```
txtstream.WriteLine("   BACKGROUND-COLOR: navy;")
txtstream.WriteLine("   FONT-FAMILY: font-family: Cambria, serif;")
txtstream.WriteLine("   FONT-SIZE: 10px;")
txtstream.WriteLine("   text-align: left;")
txtstream.WriteLine("   white-Space: nowrap;")
txtstream.WriteLine("}")
txtstream.WriteLine("span")
txtstream.WriteLine("{")
txtstream.WriteLine("   BORDER-RIGHT: #999999 3px solid;")
txtstream.WriteLine("   PADDING-RIGHT: 3px;")
txtstream.WriteLine("   PADDING-LEFT: 3px;")
txtstream.WriteLine("   FONT-WEIGHT: Normal;")
txtstream.WriteLine("   PADDING-BOTTOM: 3px;")
txtstream.WriteLine("   COLOR: white;")
txtstream.WriteLine("   PADDING-TOP: 3px;")
txtstream.WriteLine("   BORDER-BOTTOM: #999 1px solid;")
txtstream.WriteLine("   BACKGROUND-COLOR: navy;")
txtstream.WriteLine("   FONT-FAMILY: font-family: Cambria, serif;")
txtstream.WriteLine("   FONT-SIZE: 10px;")
txtstream.WriteLine("   text-align: left;")
txtstream.WriteLine("   white-Space: nowrap;")
txtstream.WriteLine("   display:inline-block;")
txtstream.WriteLine("   width: 100%;")
txtstream.WriteLine("}")
txtstream.WriteLine("textarea")
txtstream.WriteLine("{")
txtstream.WriteLine("   BORDER-RIGHT: #999999 3px solid;")
txtstream.WriteLine("   PADDING-RIGHT: 3px;")
txtstream.WriteLine("   PADDING-LEFT: 3px;")
txtstream.WriteLine("   FONT-WEIGHT: Normal;")
txtstream.WriteLine("   PADDING-BOTTOM: 3px;")
txtstream.WriteLine("   COLOR: white;")
txtstream.WriteLine("   PADDING-TOP: 3px;")
txtstream.WriteLine("   BORDER-BOTTOM: #999 1px solid;")
txtstream.WriteLine("   BACKGROUND-COLOR: navy;")
txtstream.WriteLine("   FONT-FAMILY: font-family: Cambria, serif;")
txtstream.WriteLine("   FONT-SIZE: 10px;")
txtstream.WriteLine("   text-align: left;")
txtstream.WriteLine("   white-Space: nowrap;")
txtstream.WriteLine("   width: 100%;")
```

```
txtstream.WriteLine("}")
txtstream.WriteLine("select")
txtstream.WriteLine("{")
txtstream.WriteLine("    BORDER-RIGHT: #999999 3px solid;")
txtstream.WriteLine("    PADDING-RIGHT: 6px;")
txtstream.WriteLine("    PADDING-LEFT: 6px;")
txtstream.WriteLine("    FONT-WEIGHT: Normal;")
txtstream.WriteLine("    PADDING-BOTTOM: 6px;")
txtstream.WriteLine("    COLOR: white;")
txtstream.WriteLine("    PADDING-TOP: 6px;")
txtstream.WriteLine("    BORDER-BOTTOM: #999 1px solid;")
txtstream.WriteLine("    BACKGROUND-COLOR: navy;")
txtstream.WriteLine("    FONT-FAMILY: font-family: Cambria, serif;")
txtstream.WriteLine("    FONT-SIZE: 10px;")
txtstream.WriteLine("    text-align: left;")
txtstream.WriteLine("    white-Space: nowrap;")
txtstream.WriteLine("    width: 100%;")
txtstream.WriteLine("}")
txtstream.WriteLine("input")
txtstream.WriteLine("{")
txtstream.WriteLine("    BORDER-RIGHT: #999999 3px solid;")
txtstream.WriteLine("    PADDING-RIGHT: 3px;")
txtstream.WriteLine("    PADDING-LEFT: 3px;")
txtstream.WriteLine("    FONT-WEIGHT: Bold;")
txtstream.WriteLine("    PADDING-BOTTOM: 3px;")
txtstream.WriteLine("    COLOR: white;")
txtstream.WriteLine("    PADDING-TOP: 3px;")
txtstream.WriteLine("    BORDER-BOTTOM: #999 1px solid;")
txtstream.WriteLine("    BACKGROUND-COLOR: navy;")
txtstream.WriteLine("    FONT-FAMILY: font-family: Cambria, serif;")
txtstream.WriteLine("    FONT-SIZE: 12px;")
txtstream.WriteLine("    text-align: left;")
txtstream.WriteLine("    display:table-cell;")
txtstream.WriteLine("    white-Space: nowrap;")
txtstream.WriteLine("    width: 100%;")
txtstream.WriteLine("}")
txtstream.WriteLine("h1 {")
txtstream.WriteLine("color: antiquewhite;")
txtstream.WriteLine("text-shadow: 1px 1px 1px black;")
txtstream.WriteLine("padding: 3px;")
```

```
txtstream.WriteLine("text-align: center;")
txtstream.WriteLine("box-shadow: inset 2px 2px 5px rgba(0,0,0,0.5), inset -2px
-2px 5px rgba(255,255,255,0.5);")
txtstream.WriteLine("}")
txtstream.WriteLine("</style>")
```

SHADOW BOX

```
txtstream.WriteLine("<style type='text/css'>")
txtstream.WriteLine("body")
txtstream.WriteLine("{")
txtstream.WriteLine("   PADDING-RIGHT: 0px;")
txtstream.WriteLine("   PADDING-LEFT: 0px;")
txtstream.WriteLine("   PADDING-BOTTOM: 0px;")
txtstream.WriteLine("   MARGIN: 0px;")
txtstream.WriteLine("   COLOR: #333;")
txtstream.WriteLine("   PADDING-TOP: 0px;")
txtstream.WriteLine("   FONT-FAMILY: verdana, arial, helvetica, sans-serif;")
txtstream.WriteLine("}")
txtstream.WriteLine("table")
txtstream.WriteLine("{")
txtstream.WriteLine("   BORDER-RIGHT: #999999 1px solid;")
txtstream.WriteLine("   PADDING-RIGHT: 1px;")
txtstream.WriteLine("   PADDING-LEFT: 1px;")
txtstream.WriteLine("   PADDING-BOTTOM: 1px;")
txtstream.WriteLine("   LINE-HEIGHT: 8px;")
txtstream.WriteLine("   PADDING-TOP: 1px;")
txtstream.WriteLine("   BORDER-BOTTOM: #999 1px solid;")
txtstream.WriteLine("   BACKGROUND-COLOR: #eeeeee;")
txtstream.WriteLine("
filter:progid:DXImageTransform.Microsoft.Shadow(color='silver',      Direction=135,
Strength=16)")
txtstream.WriteLine("}")
txtstream.WriteLine("th")
txtstream.WriteLine("{")
txtstream.WriteLine("   BORDER-RIGHT: #999999 3px solid;")
txtstream.WriteLine("   PADDING-RIGHT: 6px;")
txtstream.WriteLine("   PADDING-LEFT: 6px;")
txtstream.WriteLine("   FONT-WEIGHT: Bold;")
txtstream.WriteLine("   FONT-SIZE: 14px;")
```

```
txtstream.WriteLine("    PADDING-BOTTOM: 6px;")
txtstream.WriteLine("    COLOR: darkred;")
txtstream.WriteLine("    LINE-HEIGHT: 14px;")
txtstream.WriteLine("    PADDING-TOP: 6px;")
txtstream.WriteLine("    BORDER-BOTTOM: #999 1px solid;")
txtstream.WriteLine("    BACKGROUND-COLOR: #eeeeee;")
txtstream.WriteLine("    FONT-FAMILY: font-family: Cambria, serif;")
txtstream.WriteLine("    FONT-SIZE: 12px;")
txtstream.WriteLine("    text-align: left;")
txtstream.WriteLine("    white-Space: nowrap;")
txtstream.WriteLine("}")
txtstream.WriteLine(".th")
txtstream.WriteLine("{")
txtstream.WriteLine("    BORDER-RIGHT: #999999 2px solid;")
txtstream.WriteLine("    PADDING-RIGHT: 6px;")
txtstream.WriteLine("    PADDING-LEFT: 6px;")
txtstream.WriteLine("    FONT-WEIGHT: Bold;")
txtstream.WriteLine("    PADDING-BOTTOM: 6px;")
txtstream.WriteLine("    COLOR: black;")
txtstream.WriteLine("    PADDING-TOP: 6px;")
txtstream.WriteLine("    BORDER-BOTTOM: #999 2px solid;")
txtstream.WriteLine("    BACKGROUND-COLOR: #eeeeee;")
txtstream.WriteLine("    FONT-FAMILY: font-family: Cambria, serif;")
txtstream.WriteLine("    FONT-SIZE: 10px;")
txtstream.WriteLine("    text-align: right;")
txtstream.WriteLine("    white-Space: nowrap;")
txtstream.WriteLine("}")
txtstream.WriteLine("td")
txtstream.WriteLine("{")
txtstream.WriteLine("    BORDER-RIGHT: #999999 3px solid;")
txtstream.WriteLine("    PADDING-RIGHT: 6px;")
txtstream.WriteLine("    PADDING-LEFT: 6px;")
txtstream.WriteLine("    FONT-WEIGHT: Normal;")
txtstream.WriteLine("    PADDING-BOTTOM: 6px;")
txtstream.WriteLine("    COLOR: navy;")
txtstream.WriteLine("    LINE-HEIGHT: 14px;")
txtstream.WriteLine("    PADDING-TOP: 6px;")
txtstream.WriteLine("    BORDER-BOTTOM: #999 1px solid;")
txtstream.WriteLine("    BACKGROUND-COLOR: #eeeeee;")
txtstream.WriteLine("    FONT-FAMILY: font-family: Cambria, serif;")
```

```
txtstream.WriteLine("   FONT-SIZE: 12px;")
txtstream.WriteLine("   text-align: left;")
txtstream.WriteLine("   white-Space: nowrap;")
txtstream.WriteLine("}")
txtstream.WriteLine("div")
txtstream.WriteLine("{")
txtstream.WriteLine("   BORDER-RIGHT: #999999 3px solid;")
txtstream.WriteLine("   PADDING-RIGHT: 6px;")
txtstream.WriteLine("   PADDING-LEFT: 6px;")
txtstream.WriteLine("   FONT-WEIGHT: Normal;")
txtstream.WriteLine("   PADDING-BOTTOM: 6px;")
txtstream.WriteLine("   COLOR: white;")
txtstream.WriteLine("   PADDING-TOP: 6px;")
txtstream.WriteLine("   BORDER-BOTTOM: #999 1px solid;")
txtstream.WriteLine("   BACKGROUND-COLOR: navy;")
txtstream.WriteLine("   FONT-FAMILY: font-family: Cambria, serif;")
txtstream.WriteLine("   FONT-SIZE: 10px;")
txtstream.WriteLine("   text-align: left;")
txtstream.WriteLine("   white-Space: nowrap;")
txtstream.WriteLine("}")
txtstream.WriteLine("span")
txtstream.WriteLine("{")
txtstream.WriteLine("   BORDER-RIGHT: #999999 3px solid;")
txtstream.WriteLine("   PADDING-RIGHT: 3px;")
txtstream.WriteLine("   PADDING-LEFT: 3px;")
txtstream.WriteLine("   FONT-WEIGHT: Normal;")
txtstream.WriteLine("   PADDING-BOTTOM: 3px;")
txtstream.WriteLine("   COLOR: white;")
txtstream.WriteLine("   PADDING-TOP: 3px;")
txtstream.WriteLine("   BORDER-BOTTOM: #999 1px solid;")
txtstream.WriteLine("   BACKGROUND-COLOR: navy;")
txtstream.WriteLine("   FONT-FAMILY: font-family: Cambria, serif;")
txtstream.WriteLine("   FONT-SIZE: 10px;")
txtstream.WriteLine("   text-align: left;")
txtstream.WriteLine("   white-Space: nowrap;")
txtstream.WriteLine("   display: inline-block;")
txtstream.WriteLine("   width: 100%;")
txtstream.WriteLine("}")
txtstream.WriteLine("textarea")
txtstream.WriteLine("{")
```

```
txtstream.WriteLine("    BORDER-RIGHT: #999999 3px solid;")
txtstream.WriteLine("    PADDING-RIGHT: 3px;")
txtstream.WriteLine("    PADDING-LEFT: 3px;")
txtstream.WriteLine("    FONT-WEIGHT: Normal;")
txtstream.WriteLine("    PADDING-BOTTOM: 3px;")
txtstream.WriteLine("    COLOR: white;")
txtstream.WriteLine("    PADDING-TOP: 3px;")
txtstream.WriteLine("    BORDER-BOTTOM: #999 1px solid;")
txtstream.WriteLine("    BACKGROUND-COLOR: navy;")
txtstream.WriteLine("    FONT-FAMILY: font-family: Cambria, serif;")
txtstream.WriteLine("    FONT-SIZE: 10px;")
txtstream.WriteLine("    text-align: left;")
txtstream.WriteLine("    white-Space: nowrap;")
txtstream.WriteLine("    width: 100%;")
txtstream.WriteLine("}")
txtstream.WriteLine("select")
txtstream.WriteLine("{")
txtstream.WriteLine("    BORDER-RIGHT: #999999 3px solid;")
txtstream.WriteLine("    PADDING-RIGHT: 6px;")
txtstream.WriteLine("    PADDING-LEFT: 6px;")
txtstream.WriteLine("    FONT-WEIGHT: Normal;")
txtstream.WriteLine("    PADDING-BOTTOM: 6px;")
txtstream.WriteLine("    COLOR: white;")
txtstream.WriteLine("    PADDING-TOP: 6px;")
txtstream.WriteLine("    BORDER-BOTTOM: #999 1px solid;")
txtstream.WriteLine("    BACKGROUND-COLOR: navy;")
txtstream.WriteLine("    FONT-FAMILY: font-family: Cambria, serif;")
txtstream.WriteLine("    FONT-SIZE: 10px;")
txtstream.WriteLine("    text-align: left;")
txtstream.WriteLine("    white-Space: nowrap;")
txtstream.WriteLine("    width: 100%;")
txtstream.WriteLine("}")
txtstream.WriteLine("input")
txtstream.WriteLine("{")
txtstream.WriteLine("    BORDER-RIGHT: #999999 3px solid;")
txtstream.WriteLine("    PADDING-RIGHT: 3px;")
txtstream.WriteLine("    PADDING-LEFT: 3px;")
txtstream.WriteLine("    FONT-WEIGHT: Bold;")
txtstream.WriteLine("    PADDING-BOTTOM: 3px;")
txtstream.WriteLine("    COLOR: white;")
```

```
txtstream.WriteLine("    PADDING-TOP: 3px;")
txtstream.WriteLine("    BORDER-BOTTOM: #999 1px solid;")
txtstream.WriteLine("    BACKGROUND-COLOR: navy;")
txtstream.WriteLine("    FONT-FAMILY: font-family: Cambria, serif;")
txtstream.WriteLine("    FONT-SIZE: 12px;")
txtstream.WriteLine("    text-align: left;")
txtstream.WriteLine("    display: table-cell;")
txtstream.WriteLine("    white-Space: nowrap;")
txtstream.WriteLine("    width: 100%;")
txtstream.WriteLine("}")
txtstream.WriteLine("h1 {")
txtstream.WriteLine("color: antiquewhite;")
txtstream.WriteLine("text-shadow: 1px 1px 1px black;")
txtstream.WriteLine("padding: 3px;")
txtstream.WriteLine("text-align: center;")
txtstream.WriteLine("box-shadow: inset 2px 2px 5px rgba(0,0,0,0.5), inset -2px
-2px 5px rgba(255,255,255,0.5);")
txtstream.WriteLine("}")
txtstream.WriteLine("</style>")
```